Superstitions

MAX CRYER is a well-known writer, broadcaster and entertainer. In a long career, he has been a schoolteacher, a compere and television host, as well as a performer on the opera stage in London and in cabaret in Las Vegas and Hollywood. He has discussed aspects of the English language on nationwide radio in regular sessions over 20 years. Now a full-time writer living in Auckland, he has written many books, including *Is It True?*, *The Cat's Out of the Bag*, *Every Dog Has Its Day*, *Who Said That First?*, *Love Me Tender*, *The Godzone Dictionary*, *Preposterous Proverbs* and *Curious English Words and Phrases*.

Superstitions
and why we have them

Max Cryer

EXISLE
PUBLISHING

First published 2016

Exisle Publishing Limited,
P.O. Box 60-490, Titirangi, Auckland 0642, New Zealand.
'Moonrising', Narone Creek Road, Wollombi, NSW 2325, Australia.
www.exislepublishing.com

A catalogue record for this book is available from the National Library of New
Zealand.

ISBN 978-1-925335-17-0

10 9 8 7 6 5 4 3 2 1

Cover and text design by Nick Turzynski, redinc. Book Design, Auckland
Printed in China

Acknowledgements
The author thanks Paul Barrett, Graeme and Valerie Fisher,
Steve Jennings, Geoffrey Pooch and Ian Watt for their assistance in the
preparation of this book. Special thanks too to Carole Doesburg
and Richard Webster.

The person who boasts no belief at all in superstition, who wouldn't bother tossing spilled salt over the left shoulder or avoid walking under a ladder, nevertheless happily wears a wedding ring on the third finger, puts candles on their child's birthday cake, clinks glasses before a toast and says 'touch wood' when speaking of something they hope will happen. All of those are 100 per cent superstitions.

The underlying reasons for Diwali, Pesach and Ramadan still survive, as they do for Christmas and Easter. But minor 'pagan' superstitions have attached themselves to the Christmas and Easter festivals and become 'customs', amplified into massive and ruthless commercial exploitation. The ancient symbolism of decorating eggs to indicate that spring brings new life to the world, and the entirely apocryphal myth that a kind old man in Turkey threw gold coins down a chimney to help a poor Turkish family, have both been expanded into huge profit-making avalanches centred on sugar, fat and gift-giving. Thus myths and minor superstitious attachments to a more serious faith can become commercially imperative 'customs', encouraging high spending!

Consider the following:
- Why does a bride carry a bouquet?
- Do builders still have a party when the roof is put on?
- Hotel floors often go from 12 to 14 . . .
- Are opals unlucky?
- Are medals showing St Antony or St Christopher lucky?
- Do people taking part in Halloween know what it actually is?

These descendants of ancient talismans or fears are now frequently accepted into everyday life. They and many of their companion superstitions with less survival appeal are examined here.

Max Cryer

Superstition

Based on Latin *super* (above) + *stare* (to stand), joined together
as *superstare* — 'standing over'.

This came to signify:

⊚ dread and excessive fear of unseen forces, based on ignorance;

⊚ beliefs considered incompatible with truth or reason;

⊚ irrational faith in powers believed to be above the concept
of the known earth, and thus known as 'supernatural'.

abracadabra

Saying this out loud is intended to summon up strong supernatural
forces, though usually in a joking way, or in the context of show-
business 'magic'. There has been unresolved scholastic confusion
about its origin and purpose. The word emerged not long after
the time of Jesus' birth, apparently as a charm against fevers.
Some ascribe it to Hebrew, others to the more specific Aramaic
(the language Jesus spoke). Etymologist Eric Partridge hovers
between Aramaic and the equally possible Greek 'Abraxas' — an
ancient mystical word whose seven letters represent the seven
classic planets, and also the name of a Greek god with snakes for
feet. The Oxford Dictionary says that the origin is 'perhaps' the
Greek version. The truth is, nobody knows. Whatever its ancient
mystical applications in whatever language, the word is nowadays
regarded as a gimmick. The OED, ever pragmatic, dismisses it as 'a
pretended conjuring word, gibberish'.

acorn

Who knew? There is an ancient belief that a woman who constantly
carries an acorn about her person will successfully delay the
process of ageing (hers, not the acorn's). This belief relates back to
the long and sturdy life enjoyed by the oak tree . . . though the anti-
ageing process magically brought about by the acorn apparently

refers only to the woman's health and vigour. No version of the superstition asserts that the acorn has any influence on the woman's looks. True, an ancient oak tree is a mighty example of longevity, but its best friend couldn't say it looks young . . .

But from Norse mythology comes the story of how Thor found safety from thunder under an oak tree. From this grew a superstition concerning the safety value of acorns: namely, that an acorn kept on the windowsill will prevent lightning from striking the house. This is believed to be the origin of the acorn shape often used at the ends of curtain or Venetian blind cords.

Fresh acorns are credited with solving another quite different matter: when crushed into mush, some juice oozes out, which can be swallowed as a cure for drunkenness!

anglers

Recreational fishing and fishers doesn't spring to mind as a nourishing area for superstitions to grow, but they do. Depending on their locale and culture, fishers can practise the following:

- ◉ Throw back the first fish caught (whether they recognise it or not, this is based on 'appeasing the spirits').
- ◉ Cast over the left shoulder.
- ◉ Avoid changing rods between casts.
- ◉ Give a quick spit on the bait 'for luck' (to seek success by appeasing the gods).

See also **spitting**; **bumble bee**.

aphrodisiacs

In the fantasy world of superstition, the range of available aphrodisiacs is prolific. Over the centuries a wide catalogue of suggestions has accumulated, recommended to ease road bumps in the path of love/sex. At various times, the following have been vouched for:

- 11 -

leeks, apples, asparagus, potatoes, mandrake plants, dried
lizards, truffles, tomatoes, bull testicles, artichokes, parsnips,
cinnamon, salt, oysters, turnips, nutmeg, ginger, powdered rhino
horn, lettuce, marigold flowers, pepper, onions and — cabbage!

Other less straightforward candidates include:
◉ Gum from a New Guinea rosewood tree, with sulphur and
  saltpetre, wrapped and roasted.
◉ Pigeons' blood.
◉ New Zealand stag antlers ground up.

Some Moroccan men believe that eating an egg every morning for
forty days leads to improved sexual performance. Or — if you're
more stoic — in some circles dried periwinkle flowers mixed with
powdered earthworms has been highly recommended.

apples

There is no mention of apples
in the Bible's story of Adam
and Eve, but the misperception
persists that disaster struck
them when one was eaten. In
parts of America, if there is
sunshine on Christmas Day, this
foretells that the apple crops will be
generous the following year. Watch out, however, if the
trees bloom before autumn — this means someone's
death is near. For the unwed, many superstitions
exist to help foretell their future, and one featuring
an apple is intriguing. Peel an apple in one long
continuous strip, then throw the peel backward
over the left shoulder. When it falls on the ground,
the shape made by the peel will be the initial of the
thrower's future wife or husband.

April Fool's Day

For centuries, the 'New Year' celebrations had been observed on 1 April, although the real civil and legal new year was marked on what would now be 25 March. But that was Lady Day, during Holy Week, hence the delay to a week or so later.

When the Gregorian calendar was adopted (the one we have now) the New Year occurred on 1 January, but legend tells that peasant folk in Europe were not always keen on this change. In festive array, they would turn up at their neighbours ready to party, jokingly trying to convince them that 1 April was still the New Year. This amiable trickery spread and became an adventure in testing the patience, alertness and humour of anyone and everyone.

But a belief has crept in that the fooling has to stop at midday: bad luck will come to anyone who tries to perpetrate an April Fools trick after 12 noon.

apron

Although innocently hanging on the kitchen door, the humble apron has more power in superstition than one might think. For instance, putting it on back to front by mistake will bring good luck. But remember — if it's been put on the correct way and things start going astray during the day, taking the apron off and putting it back on *deliberately* back-to-front, will reverse the day's rhythm and calm will be restored.

As a bonus, anyone wearing an apron when getting their first glimpse of a new moon should immediately make a wish, then rapidly take the apron off and put it on back-to-front. This ensures that the wish will come true.

asthma

Antihistamines might help, but in their absence, the superstitious can provide three other remedies to help bring relief:

1. In ancient Rome the advised cure was to eat 20 crickets soaked in wine.
2. Cornish folk recommended rolling cobwebs into a ball, then swallowing it.
3. Lost in time, a sure cure was believed to be to drink foam from the mouth of a donkey.

baking bread at Christmas

It seems unlikely to occur during a modern Christmas, but a diligent householder baking bread at Christmas (and believing in superstitions) is protecting the household from accident, misfortune and fire for the following year. Furthermore, the baker who abides by superstition will believe that bread baked on Christmas Day, when crumbled into hot water, will help cure dysentery and diarrhoea.

See also **bread**.

baptism

The ceremony of giving a baby its name dates back to what are known as pagan times. A new-born baby was vulnerable — its body and soul could be invaded by evil spirits and witches. Protection was acquired by being sure the cradle contained some garlic, iron and salt, and having a naming ceremony.

When the baby's name was decided, it was kept totally secret. Even the child itself was not addressed by the name, in case some passing witch learned the new baby's name and was able to cast spells against it. Naming ceremonies took place as soon as possible, with ritual incantations and purified water.

baldness

In spite of extensive advertising claims to the contrary, most men afflicted by baldness find the condition irreversible. An America superstition claims that baldness can be delayed by cutting the existing hair very short, then singeing the cut ends. Another superstition claims that when a man starts to go bald, he can slow the process by stuffing cyclamen leaves up his nose. And sprinkling parsley seeds on the head three times a year is also believed to help.

Three other cures have come down to us from ancient traditions — albeit two of them might be rather difficult to obtain:

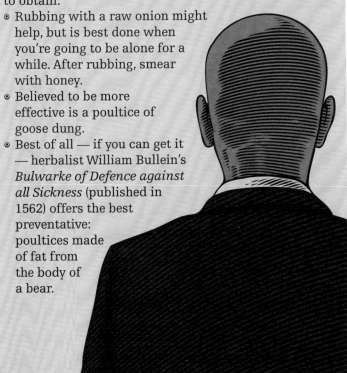

- Rubbing with a raw onion might help, but is best done when you're going to be alone for a while. After rubbing, smear with honey.
- Believed to be more effective is a poultice of goose dung.
- Best of all — if you can get it — herbalist William Bullein's *Bulwarke of Defence against all Sickness* (published in 1562) offers the best preventative: poultices made of fat from the body of a bear.

In later centuries, versions of the 'baby naming' ceremony were absorbed into the newer Christian event also known as baptism or christening.

See also **christening**.

basil

It's usually not difficult to grow, but apart from its delicious usefulness in cooking, superstitions claim that basil has somewhat ambiguous effects on your life. The ancient Greeks considered it brought bad luck — and could also cause hatred. Italians, on the other hand, saw it as representing love.

In some parts of India a leaf of basil was placed on someone recently dead, as it would help the departed one's spirit to reach the afterlife. But in frightening contrast, herbalist Thomas Culpepper (1563) reported an ancient French belief that if one sniffed the leaves of basil, a scorpion would grow inside your brain! However, if you actually *want* a pet scorpion, just place basil leaves under a pot plant — and a scorpion will grow there (instead of inside the brain).

Although there is no known evidence, the belief persists that when Herod's stepdaughter danced for the head of John the Baptist, and was awarded it, she kept the head in a bowl of basil leaves — to avoid the smell. (By the way, the name Salome for Herod's stepdaughter is not in the Bible at all. Nor is there any mention of her dancing with seven veils.)

bay

Besides giving their flavour to cooking, bay tree leaves have had a busy history. To ancient Romans the bay tree symbolised victory and its leaves were a protection against evil — especially witches and ghosts. Winners were crowned with it, and its branches adorned houses to bring good luck. Placed beneath a night-time pillow, bay leaves were believed to help bring pleasant dreams, and some leaves carried about in one's clothing would continue to fend off evil spirits.

A bay tree planted near a house would ward off infections, and there was a bonus belief that lightning would not strike a bay tree but would divert away from it. The Roman Emperor Tiberius is reported to have always donned a crown made of bay leaves when thunderous weather threatened, in order that any lightning would be diverted from his royal person. Tiberius died when he was 78, not from lightning, but reportedly after being smothered by enemies.

bed

For those who are unmarried, a superstition might offer some help. It concerns 'turning' or 'making' a bed each day:

If one day you would be wed,
Turn your bed from foot to head.

Married or not, the superstitious abide by the belief that whatever side of the bed you get into at night is the side you *must* get out of in the morning. Not doing so will cause disruption. In fact, the belief resulted in the saying that someone disgruntled 'got out the wrong side of the bed'. (However, any potential disruption caused by inadvertently getting out on the 'wrong' side can be averted by putting one's socks on the right foot first, then the left.)

The jury is still out on the ancient and vexed superstition regarding getting out of bed 'backwards'. One school of thought decrees it to be bad luck, but the opposition says it is good luck. It's probably best avoided by getting out of bed frontwards.

bells

A recurring belief among superstitions is that noise drives away evil spirits. Long before the establishment of Christian churches, the sound of bells and other created noises were used to defeat the attentions of unwelcome and bad spirit beings. Those who believed witches could fly on broomsticks were sure that the sound of bells caused witches to fall off.

A form of this belief transferred to the use of bells in churches during the early centuries of Christianity, and the not uncommon use of smaller bells being rung during the actual service. Another belief was that the pealing of bells during thunderstorms would help prevent damage. Sociology author E. M. Leather reports an eighth-century church blessing whereby bells were to protect people from 'the shadow of phantoms, the assault of whirlwinds, the stroke of lightning, the harm of thunder, and the injurie of tempests'.

See also **toast**; **New Year's Eve**.

best man
At a wedding, the 'groomsmen' and their leader, the 'best man', originally protected the bride from any marauding rival of the groom's who wished to capture and deliver her to the aforementioned rival.

Another way of protecting the bride was for the best man and groomsmen to wear a small bunch of flowers and herbs, in order to ward off any lurking evil spirits who had designs on upsetting the wedding ceremony. The foliage was worn on their left side, near the heart — and from the old superstition the 'custom' remains in the men's floral 'buttonholes'.

birthdays
The belief that a person's life and fortune, ill or otherwise, is governed by the conjunction of the stars at the hour, day and month of their birth still has many flourishing survivors. Constant

birds

Unrest is felt in many households if a bird should fly in through an open window, then fly out again. It is the signal that a family death is imminent. Outside the house, anyone hit by bird droppings (and who hasn't been?) can choose between two superstitions:
1. Expect bad luck in the near future.
2. Good luck will now come to you.

Take your pick.

features in magazines and newspapers acknowledge this.

A simpler belief is the ancient superstition which focuses on the day the birth takes place. There is a difficulty in taking it seriously, as it all depends on which side of the International Date Line you live. One person's Monday birth could be another person's Sunday or Tuesday elsewhere. There are a dozen variations on the prediction, the most frequently heard being:

Monday's child is fair of face,
Tuesday's child is full of grace,
Wednesday's child is full of woe,
Thursday's child has far to go,
Friday's child is loving and giving,
Saturday's child works hard for a living,
But the child that is born on the Sabbath Day
Is blithe and bonny, good and gay.

The evolution of language has cast a different perspective on Sunday's child.

birthday cake

Historically, birthdays haven't always been celebrated as they are now. In some cultures, women's and children's birthdays weren't celebrated at all. But now that they are, the custom of the cake with candles is following a ritualised superstitious belief from ancient Greece.

Other cultures have celebrated birthdays by roasting an ox — or something smaller for those less wealthy. But among the many gods and goddesses worshipped by the Greeks was Artemis — goddess of the moon. Her birthday was celebrated by preparing round cakes like a full moon. And because the moon glows with light, the cakes were decorated with lighted candles on top, so the circular glowing cake resembled the moon. A parallel superstition was that by blowing out the candles, the smoke would go upwards carrying a wish to the moon.

Over thousands of years, the ancient connection between the moon and its governance of wishes has faded away, and sometimes birthday cakes are no longer round. However, the cake with glowing candles to be blown out, accompanied by a wish, has survived as a custom, even if the superstition behind it is seldom acknowledged.

black cats *See* cats

Black Friday

Severe apprehension affects many people when the 13th day of a month falls on a Friday. Those sensitive to superstition find the combination particularly nerve-wracking, as it combines the bad vibes already existing about any Friday with the number 13.

The 'Friday' part of the equation is difficult to explain. While it is popularly believed that Jesus was crucified on a Friday, there is absolutely no evidence that this was the case. The Bible doesn't come anywhere near designating the day, and close study and complex reasoning applied to the biblical texts can only come up with Wednesday, Thursday or Friday as the *possible* crucifixion dates. Nevertheless, in spite of the scholastic confusion, a widespread assumption exists that Friday has an aura of evil, because of the possibility that Jesus was crucified on that day.

Although Friday and 13 separately have their own quotient of superstitions, the two components appeared not to combine until the middle of the nineteenth century. The composer Gioachino Rossini was known to regard both Friday and 13 as unlucky. After he died in 1868, the biography published the following year noted that his death had occurred on Friday the 13th. This was the first known coupling of the two factors.

In the following decades, the bad odour of the conjunction appeared to have taken sufficient root for T. W. Lawson's 1907 novel, *Friday the Thirteenth*, to have some resonance. It depicted a businessman creating a financial upheaval on the share market by manipulating severe apprehension about the date of Friday the 13th.

Other superstitions involving this particular date include:
- If you change your bedding on Friday the 13th, prepare for the bad dreams this will bring you.
- Cutting your hair on Friday the 13th can cause death to a member of your family.
- A new business started on Friday the 13th will soon be bankrupt.

In the early 1990s, American psychotherapist Dr Donald Dossey, a specialist in phobia and stress management, invented a word for the fear of Friday the 13th: paraskevidekatriaphobia. He is reputed to have said that when someone was able to pronounce the word, they were cured of their fear!

See also **days**; **Friday**; **thirteen**.

blackheads

Acne is often the curse of the teenage years, but according to ancient superstition, one way of curing blackheads is to bend a wild bramble bush into an arch shape, make the bent-down end firm, then crawl through the arch three times. The seriously devout believe this will also cure dysentery and boils.

bones

Bones were long assumed to contain some essence of the soul. Human bones, when no longer required by their owner, figure in some superstitions of a medical nature. For example, someone beset with cramps should carry with them the knee bone of a man (who has no further use for it). Having a knucklebone somewhere among the clothes you are wearing is believed to help with the same complaint. And a hopeful cure for dysentery is to drink powdered bones mixed with red wine. Something more serious, like gout, needs a plaster made from earth scraped from a previously buried human shin bone. A person with too many headaches can slow them down by sniffing moss which has grown on a deceased person's skull, and epileptics will respond to that skull being grated and added to their normal food.

Natives of Australia upheld the concept of a bone containing power, and the ancient ceremony of 'pointing the bone' was a ritualised death warrant. That the pointing often appeared to cause death suggests that the powerful psychosomatic effect on the person being pointed at virtually compelled the victim to self-will their own demise, in recognition of the ancient superstitious ritual.

See also **headache**.

bread

Even in modern times, the expressions 'breadwinner' and 'on the breadline' convey how important the basic sustenance of bread has always been considered a symbol of financial capability and survival. But those sensitive to superstition must observe:

- Bread should not be baked at all if there is a dead person still in the house.
- An old Welsh superstition warns if baked bread has cracks or holes, someone in the family will soon die.
- While bread is baking, the person cooking it must not sing.
- A loaf must always be on the table in its upright position — if it falls on its side, bad luck will ensue.
- Worse — if a loaf is placed on the table upside down, bad luck comes to all sitting there.
- If a buttered slice falls on the floor, buttered side up, expect a visitor soon.
- A single woman, if she takes the last slice of bread from a plate, will remain single.
- A single man who takes the last slice will marry a woman with a fortune.
- But if a male or female is *offered* the last slice and takes it, love and fortune will come to them.
- Young lads who aspire to having a hairy chest can achieve this by eating a lot of bread.
- In the west of England, small boys are warned to stay away when dough is being kneaded, in case someone kneading gives them a pat with a floury hand, in which case the boy will never grow a beard.
- In Kentucky, stirring the bread-making mix towards you is bad luck; stirring away from you is believed to bring good luck.

See also **baking bread at Christmas**.

break a leg

This is a superstition normally said to someone when you *don't* want them to break a leg, such as just before they walk on stage to perform, or are due to make an important speech to a distinguished gathering. The origin appears to be German. According to Baron von Richtofen's biography, the phrase 'Hals und Beinbruch' ('neck and leg fracture') was commonly used by German pilots in World War Two to wish each other luck before a flight. The English version seems to have passed from German through Yiddish into English, and is a 'contrary superstition' — in that what you are saying is the opposite of what you hope to occur. It's a little like taking an umbrella out with you to ensure that there'll be no rain.

bridal bouquet

Fresh flowers are required because of the ancient superstition that they will bring fertility to the forthcoming union. It is especially beneficial if orange blossoms are included, as these blooms are renowned for bringing the bride and groom children. Another less frequently observed superstition advises the bride to include some garlic in her bouquet as well (though for obvious reasons, not too much). This will be a back-up to the veil in helping keep evil demons away.

The joyous and seemingly innocent custom of 'throwing the bouquet' is a custom developed from an old superstition. In centuries past, a belief grew that the happiness of the new bride could be passed on to wedding guests — if they could secure a fragment of her bridal dress. Over time this tended to become a free-for-all attempt to tear pieces away from the dress, sometimes devolving into a snatch-and-grab which tended to get out of hand.

Gradually a gentler version evolved: passing on the bridal happiness by throwing the wedding bouquet over the guests. The woman who caught it would thus believe — as the old superstition promised — that she would share the bride's good fortune and would herself soon marry.

bridal veil

The veil is still commonly worn by brides in one style or another. Whatever the style or length, it is the manifestation of an ancient superstition that a veil hides the bride from evil demons.

bridegroom

Why 'groom?' Back in the sixth century, the Old English word *guma* meant 'man', so a *brydguma* was 'the bride's man'. By the year 1200 the word *guma* had modified into *grome*, so the man standing next to the bride was a *brydgrome*. Gentle spelling shifts then took place until the 1600s, when *bridegroom* settled into place — and remains to this day.

In the 1800s the word 'groom' gained an extra meaning of a person who attends horses. This was unrelated to the original meaning of a man who walks up the aisle single and comes back married. Curry-combing manes and tails is not included in the duties expected of a man who is acquiring a wife.

bride on the left of the groom

While this is not obligatory, it is the usual custom for the bride to be at her husband's left when the couple walk from the altar to wherever the register is to be signed, and when they leave a Christian church and walk along the passageway through the central nave (known as the 'aisle', though church architectural tradition disagrees, and says it is not the church's 'aisle'). The custom dates back to the superstitious necessity for the groom to have his right-hand free for his sword — in case any potential abductor storms in with an eye on the bride.

brides

Wearing white is based on the ancient symbolism of that colour representing innocence and purity — or to put it bluntly, virginity. Even if the latter is not the case, this can be overridden by the bride wearing a silk fabric (which they usually do), as this attracts good luck to her and her future. However, she should avoid satin. For some unknown reason, superstition frowns on it because it creates an aura of bad luck! Velvet is also a no-no: to the superstitious it signifies that poverty lies just ahead.

A bride is usually wearing her wedding dress for the first time, so it is essential that it be examined very carefully for any pins that may have been left in accidentally. Not just because one might scratch her, but because such pins cast bad luck on the future of the marriage.

On the other hand, including pearls somewhere in the ensemble either encourages good luck to smile upon the day, or signals that there will be tears during the marriage. Superstition is often what scientists refer to as a variable.

bridesmaids

Apart from looking good, and rearranging the bride's veil when a Christian ceremony reaches its high point, the maids no longer fulfil the original belief which put them there. In very early days, the young women accompanying the bride positioned themselves to conceal and protect her, because of a superstition that if she were unprotected an evil demon might get in on the act and upset the rhythm of what should be a happy occasion.

In addition, if a rival of the groom's actually wanted to marry the woman intending to say 'Yes' to the groom, again there was danger of him mounting a posse to come and purloin the bride before the marriage, thus rendering her no longer available to the rival. So the 'maids' were not just decorative, but also actively protective.

But the popularity of a bride's young friends may be their undoing in the marriage stakes: ancient superstition decrees that any woman who does bridesmaid duties three times will never get married herself.

But there is a user-friendly superstition which can remedy the problem: if she takes bridesmaid duties four more times, the magic figure of seven ensures she *will* get married.

See also **best man**.

brimstone

'Brimstone' is an old name for sulphur — a yellow chemical, often in crystal form, which burns with a mysterious-looking blue flame. Homoeopathist John Henry Clarke in his *Materia Media* (1900) reports the superstition that if you suffer from cramps, carrying a lump of sulphur around with you will provide protection against their occurrence. At night, sewn into a very thin bag and placed inside the bedclothes or under the mattress, the sulphur's reputation is that it will also prevent dreaded nocturnal muscle cramps.

See also **bones**.

bumble bee

Over the centuries, superstitions developed around bumble bees. In parts of the United Kingdom it has long been believed that catching the first bumble bee in spring and taking it with you when you go fishing will help you catch many fish.

Another superstition maintains that if a bumble bee flies into your house, there's a choice:
- You're about to have an unexpected visitor.
- Bad luck is coming to the house soon.
- Good luck is coming to the house soon.

bunion

If you suffer from this painful enlargement and repositioning of a toe, forget surgery and find a friendly farmer. An ancient superstition assures us that bunion sufferers do not need a doctor; all they need is a poultice of cow dung mixed with fish oil, and the bunion and its pain will vanish overnight.

burn

Similarly, if a burn is painful (they usually are) another rural superstition comes to the rescue. Rub the burn area with goose dung which has been fried in butter.

butterflies

Some superstitions would have us believe that butterflies are actually the souls of the dear departed, transformed into something beautiful but fragile. This is a warning that no butterfly should ever be killed — it may be one of your relatives, or a dear friend, in a new form!

However, to see three butterflies together is distinctly bad news, and to see one flying about during the night is especially disastrous: it is an already departed soul alerting you that you will be the next to go.

See also **three — a lucky number?**

candle

For centuries the candle-flame has engendered mystique. Superstitious ancient Egyptians sat in a south-facing cave gazing into a candle-flame until an image of a god could be ascertained. Sleep followed, with the 'flame-summoned' deity answering questions put by the dreaming sleeper. Lit candles still have a place in the ceremonies of contemporary religions, a custom surviving from an ancient superstition, which has lasted several millennia, that a candle-flame drives away evil spirits.

But in the home environment, if a candle proves difficult to light it could be telling you that rain is coming soon. And blowing out a candle-flame follows a well-known superstition which plays a prominent part in many modern birthday parties.

See also **cigarettes; birthday cake.**

card players

The superstition attached to the nine of diamonds playing card ('the curse of Scotland' presaging very bad luck for whoever is dealt it) has a disputed origin. Its 'curse factor' is thought to have arisen because in 1692 the Earl of Stair was significant in launching the brutal and infamous massacre of the Highlanders . . . and his family crest bore a strong similarity to the nine of diamonds playing card. The four of clubs is believed by many to be bad news for any hand into which it is dealt — and the curse is particularly potent if the four of clubs is dealt as the first card of the session. This four of clubs card is often called 'the devil's bedstead' (or 'the devil's bedpost' or 'the devil's four-poster').

Cards showing spades can cause unrest because they show too much black, which is associated with death. One of the most dramatic moments in the operatic repertoire is when Bizet's Carmen (1875) is having her fortune told and turns over a spade — and immediately fears that her death is impending. In the later stage musical version (*Carmen Jones*, 1943), a much bigger deal is made of the card she turns up: the nine of spades. And indeed, in the opera and the musical, not long after the card game Carmen dies an ignominious death.

Some card superstitions don't apply to the actual cards:
- Playing on an uncovered surface: Superstition has it that ill results await the player who engages in a game of cards on a bare table rather than on one covered by cloth.
- Picking up and examining one's cards before the dealer has finished delivering them to all the players.
- Sitting cross-legged: One is, after all, making a cross and therefore working a hex sign on oneself. (But some players regard sitting cross-legged as bringing good luck. Take your pick.)
- Whistling or singing: this will draw bad luck to the player.
- If there's a dog in the room, it will bring bad luck to players.

And for good luck, try the following:
- A gentle blowing: while shuffling, some breath upon the deck makes it deal good cards for you.
- If your luck's been bad, change seats. If this is not possible, turn your chair around and sit astride it. (And slipping a handkerchief between your bottom and the seat helps lessen contact with the 'unlucky chair'.)

cats

Ancient Egyptians gave cats the status of gods. They also considered the number three to be a magical trinity, even holy. The cat was so esteemed that the symmetry of the holy 'three' was magnified by endowing the cat's life with the concept of multiplying *three by three* into an awesome nine. An extra factor was probably admiration for the cat's flexibility and speed of movement. That mythical consideration of a cat having nine lives went into history and became universally accepted, right down to the present day. But of course cats have only one life, like everything else.

Other cat superstitions haven't survived so well. Nowadays few people believe that a black cat is actually a witch who is able to assume animal form. And ignoring ancient caution, today family matters are often discussed when a cat is in the room, disregarding an old belief that the cat could be an evil presence in disguise, eavesdropping in order to learn secrets.

Then there are the medical cat superstitions:
- ⊚ If toothache is slow to leave, send it on its way by finding the dried skin of a dead cat and holding it next to the painful area.
- ⊚ But when a debilitating sickness affects someone, wash the patient's body carefully, keep the water — and throw it over a cat! The cat will escape elsewhere very quickly — and take the sickness with it.

A most unreliable superstition applies to the black cat. In some countries (for example, Britain and Japan) a black cat crossing your path is considered very good luck, but quite the reverse applies in other countries, such as the United States, where the same cat crossing your path implies the worst possible bad luck. (Legend also has it that Napoleon was fearful of black cats.) The jury is out on which of the superstitions is valid — or perhaps neither. The wise words of the late Groucho Marx could put that belief in a more pragmatic perspective:

A black cat crossing your path signifies that the animal is going somewhere.

Christmas

The basis of this festival is a widespread acknowledgement and celebration of the birth of Jesus, in which superstition plays no part. Several hundred years after his death, lack of knowledge about the actual time of his birth resulted in the establishment of a 'commemoration date' of 25 December, which has remained the celebration date ever since.

Some of the Christmas festive activities have pre-Christian origins from a Druid or 'pagan' environment, and came into being in the northern hemisphere winter — before sailing ships, then aeroplanes, opened up the other half of the world where the day falls in midsummer. But December has been successful — retaining midwinter ambience in one hemisphere and an equally festive midsummer ambience in the other.

Whether of pagan origin or not, most of the customs which have evolved around Christmas have little or no reference to supernatural causes. Christmas superstitions existed in past centuries, but many have now become disregarded. For example:

- Opening the doors of the house at midnight on Christmas Eve in order to expel any evil spirits — at the same time lighting a candle in the hope that it would continue to burn though the dark hours until dawn, thus ensuring the household's prosperity.
- A persistent rural superstition had it that all cattle developed the power of speech at midnight on Christmas Eve. This was never proven or disproven — because the superstition decreed that it would be fatal for any human to actually hear them.

Several old superstitions are based around Christmastime eating. It was believed that:

- Good health in the coming year would be secured by eating an apple on Christmas Eve.
- The number of mince pies eaten on Christmas Day would result in future happiness for the same number of months.
- Furthermore, to some believers Christmas Day dinner had to consist of nine dishes — with fish scales placed under each plate — to bring good luck.

Nevertheless, the actual commemoration of Jesus' birth continues with sincerity and mainly without any of these old beliefs. But in some ways the fading of superstitions from the past has been replaced by other imperatives. Multiple business enterprises have invented flagrant commercial interests for 'the Christmas season' which have nothing to do with the actual meaning of Christmas. The inclination to worship is overshadowed by the imperative to spend, in a colourful, profit-making circus described by author Joe Bennett as 'the smiley face on the piranha of commerce'.

chair

The humble chair has a superstition of its own. When a visitor leaves the house and, maybe out of politeness, moves their chair back to its original place in the room, they will never visit that house again.

Christmas cake

A long-held superstition that Christmas cake should be eaten on Christmas Eve has been displaced by customarily eating it on Christmas Day.

Christmas cards

They were invented in 1843 and have developed into a widely observed custom, with no superstitious influence. Quite the reverse in fact — seeing their prevalence growing, the printing trade gradually edged Christmas out of the equation, and made available greeting cards which fitted into the 'sending cards' custom of a December holiday — but with no mention of Christianity. Thus cards simply saying 'Happy Holidays' or 'Festive Greetings' could be bought and sent by Hindus, Jews, Buddhists and indeed worshippers of any kind. In other words, a bigger market.

Christmas decorations

Quite apart from its religious significance, Christmas has become the focus of superstitions about the decorations traditional to the season.

One of the many customs which have been engendered in the name of Christianity is the prescribed date for taking down a household's Christmas decorations. It is connected with the ubiquitous 'twelve days of Christmas' (a concept largely ignored or forgotten, especially in the southern hemisphere where summer's Christmas 'holiday season' lasts until February). The

legend regarding decorations maintains that decorations must be taken down on the twelfth day of Christmas. For those who've forgotten, this is 6 January.

This is based on a superstition which decrees that taking decorations down before 6 January can endanger the household's prosperity in the coming year. But bad luck will also be drawn to a household which leaves its decorations up *after* the twelfth day. So there is no choice: take the decorations down *on* the twelfth day.

But there's more: keeping one sprig of (genuine) evergreen for the coming year will aid the household's prosperity. And here you can take your pick between two superstitions: either (1) the remaining evergreen decorations should be burned; or (2) the remaining evergreens should never be burned.

Apart from remembering the details, one has to observe that these superstitions applied mainly to the era of BP — Before Plastic. In some parts of the world genuine ivy, mistletoe and holly are simply not available, but may be represented by polyvinyl-acetate — which is often considered more convenient anyway. And burning doesn't come into it . . . those decorations are stashed away in an obscure cupboard, emerge twelve months later and, after a quick dusting, look exactly as they did a year earlier.

Christmas pudding

The superstition that the Christmas pudding should be stirred from east to west and by every member of the household has largely been supplanted by the belief that it is easier to buy one from the supermarket. However, there could be a problem if the household includes an unmarried woman. Because the pudding has been bought she will not get her turn at stirring, and superstition dictates that if she does not stir a pudding at all she will not be wearing a bridal veil for at least another year.

One superstition which has survived, at least among home-made puddings, is that a silver coin cooked in the mix will bestow luck on the person whose serving of the pudding contains the coin.

Christmas trees

Christmas trees are a custom with a pragmatic history which has no hint of the supernatural. They date back to the centuries-old pre-Christian custom of bringing a small evergreen tree into the house at midwinter, as a reminder that green leaves will return to the land when winter eases into spring. Decorating it became normal; the presents came much later. German-born Queen Charlotte introduced English royals to her homeland's version of the Christmas tree in 1800, and later her granddaughter Victoria was delighted to have her own tree when she was thirteen.

christening

The two terms 'baptism' and 'christening' are often perceived as interchangeable. But the word 'christening' is from the Greek **christos** meaning 'anointed', and 'christening' has the purpose of bringing a child into one of the specified divisions within Christianity, usually with a ceremony involving water. In other respects 'christening' and 'baptism' are similar: a ceremony of initiation and dedication. A baby is 'baptised' during a 'christening' service, just as people are 'married' during a 'wedding' service.

See also **baptism**.

cigarettes

While avoiding using one match for three cigarettes was certainly associated with the Boer War and World War One, the superstitious resistance towards lighting of three flames from one source pre-dates both those wars, and also the invention of cigarettes, by hundreds of years.

Many superstitions surround the use of candles, from the times when they were the principal source of domestic light. Now that this is no longer the case, most of the legends and beliefs about them have faded away, with the exception of the 'three flames' superstition, which has adapted itself to modern cigarette circumstances.

For centuries it was a widely observed superstition that lighting three candles from one taper was an invitation to doom. In fact, three candles burning in a group was to be avoided, since misfortune would be the outcome. F. S. L. Lyons' biography of Irish politician Charles Parnell tells that in 1880 when Parnell was not well, a friend visited him in his bedroom, which was lit by four candles. When one candle guttered and died, Parnell raised himself and blew out another, explaining to the visitor that since three candles burning would bring severe misfortune, it would be better to make do with just two.

The transition of the superstition from 'candle' to 'cigarette' acknowledged the genuine danger of being visible during modern warfare, and was a fine example of an ancient belief being adapted to changed circumstances.

cobwebs

The main superstition surrounding cobwebs has a certain practicality and indeed some merit — that thick cobwebs applied to a wound will slow down and even stop the bleeding. There is apparently some truth in this, provided the wound is not too deep and the cobweb not too dusty and unhygienic. Historically housewives were known to keep one cupboard web-draped, in case a bleeding wound needed to be staunched.

In parts of America, seeing cobwebs growing in the grass signifies the onset of rain. Another American superstition warns that if a young woman finds a cobweb on her door, it signifies that the young man she believes is courting her is also calling on another young woman!

See also **asthma; spiders**.

coffee

Interpreting the 'significance' of left-over leaves in a just-drunk cup of tea is formally called tasseomancy. However, a related American superstition reveals the signals which can be seen in a cup of coffee. The bubbles floating on top of coffee can be significant: if they drift towards the drinker, then good fortune is coming soon.

Of equal importance are images discernible in any grounds left after drinking a cup of coffee (real coffee, not instant). A diligent reader of coffee grounds can find nearly a hundred images at the bottom of the cup, each of which can be interpreted to the drinker as foretelling their future.

confetti

For thousands of years, various cultures maintained the superstition that rice and other grains, such as wheat or corn, were symbolic of encouraging fertility. Long before weddings took the shape they have now, grains were thrown at a newly married couple in the belief that this would help them have children.

Indian and Arabic cultures often used fennel and coriander seeds — which did double duty as sweets to nibble. Occasionally sugar-coated grains of rice were used. When these practices filtered through to Europe, the custom modified to throwing actual small sweets. These became known by the Latin word for a sweet, *confectum*, which in Italian became *confetto*, plural *confetti* — so Italians were throwing real sweets at wedding couples.

A version of the custom then came to England. A 1665 account records the throwing of wheat over newlyweds, again to signify hope that the outcome of the wedding would prove as fertile as the wheat grains. In later centuries, rice and even flowers were often substituted in England. Over time, when flowers and sweets were hard to obtain or too expensive, small bits of coloured paper became an acceptable substitute. But the name confetti (little sweets) still remained, though their superstitious significance of conveying successful fertility is seldom mentioned.

Confetti's historical association with fertility has discreetly morphed into a more genteel belief that the shower of confetti symbolises the 'good gifts' with which the throwers hope the couple's married life will be blessed. It has become a pleasant custom, which people carry out without really knowing why.

cough

An ancient superstition aims to provide an inexpensive cure for a persistent cough: a drink of barley water in which three snails have been gently boiled.

cows

The normal sweetness of cows' breath may not be familiar to those living outside rural areas, but there is an interesting belief associated with it. Legend has it that as baby Jesus lay in the manger, a cow saw him shiver with cold. She moved towards Jesus, breathed warm air over him and, with her mouth, gently edged some hay over the now not-so-cold baby. Her reward was that the breath of all her descendants for ever after would be sweet.

Another more serious quality once assigned to cows' breath was that it could cure tuberculosis. One casualty thereof was famous writer Katherine Mansfield, who was 'treated' in France by the theosopher George Gurdjieff, who assured her that the breath of cows would banish her (advanced) tuberculosis. In 1922 she wrote of 'a high couch in the stable where I may sit and inhale their breath.' Two months later she died.

Another less serious belief — alas also discredited — claimed that cows dislike the sound of anybody singing in the milking shed. Once radio was invented, many dairy farmers had it playing in their shed during milking, with no known deleterious effects from the sound of singing.

cramps

Wise doctors and experienced physiotherapists despair of being able to farewell night-time cramps. Throughout history, pills and potions have frequently been disregarded in favour of superstitious practices to prevent the pain, including:
- Several wine-corks inside a cut-off stocking foot, kept under the sheets in no particular place.
- A ring made from a coffin handle.
- A lump of sulphur in a little bag, placed between the sheets.
- A nutmeg in the bed.
- A garter made from an eel's skin.

If these fail and the cramps strike:

⊚ Eat a banana.
⊚ Or swallow a spoonful of mustard.
⊚ Or drink some cider vinegar.
⊚ Or rub the cramped area with a steel spoon kept close by.

Good luck !

See also **bones**; **brimstone**; **iron**; **shoes**.

cross fingers

There is an ancient belief that two people linking index fingers to represent a solemn wish have a greater chance of the wish coming true because the two linked fingers symbolically capture the wish and help bring it to fruition.

Over centuries, the need for two people to perform the 'wish' ritual diminished, and it became a solo — just linking the forefinger over the next (middle) finger while wishing or hoping. The fact that two linked fingers roughly formed the shape of a cross, and that just one person was involved in crossing them, helped the superstition ease into Christian acceptance.

Within Christian tradition, the word 'cross' and its image have grown to be significant of many qualities associated with Jesus. The fact that folding one finger over another does not really resemble a cross is of little consequence, but it became significant historically. During times when Christians were being persecuted, the crossing of fingers was a secret sign for Christians to recognise others of the same faith. The overlapping of one finger did duty as a 'cross' — and wasn't too obvious to the persecutors.

From this arose the superstitious beliefs about two people crossing their index fingers, then of one person crossing two of their own fingers, practices which are now customary among both Christians and non-Christians. Crossing fingers invokes a kind of protection — including some form of divine intervention which prevents a person to whom you are telling a lie from identifying that it is a lie — if you hold your crossed fingers behind your back while lying.

Despite all of this, it is not uncommon to say the phrase 'cross fingers' without actually doing it.

d

daddy-long-legs

The spindly daddy-long-legs is greeted fairly amiably in Britain, where many believe that if you refrain from harming them the year's crops will be bounteous. They are treated equally amiably in America where, according to one superstition, they can assist a farmer to find his stock if it wanders. Say to the daddy-long-legs, 'Grand-daddy, where did my cows go?' and the creature will lift one slender leg and point it in the direction the farmer must go to find them.

A minor trans-Atlantic confusion needs to be clarified, however. The two nations use the same name for entirely different creatures. The British daddy-long-legs (correctly called the crane fly) is a spindly insect with six legs. In America the daddy-long-legs (also known as the harvestman) is an arachnid, with eight legs.

daisy

Saying 'she/he loves me, she/he loves me not' as you pluck alternate daisy petals is a familiar youthful pastime. The petal left at the end is the harbinger of requited love — or a solo life. Mind you, superstition decrees that this petal-plucking ritual is only effective if done at midday, when facing towards the sun.

The daisy is also believed to provide an alternative way of predicting a marital future: dig up some daisy roots and sleep with them under the pillow. A vision of your future partner will come to you in a dream . . . or not.

days

In spite of changes over the centuries to what we know as the calendar, various folklore beliefs and superstitions remained intact. They just adjusted to the day of the month which a 'new' calendar bestowed on an 'old' calendar.

Monday didn't come out very well. Three ancient superstitions (based on no evidence) still surround it:
- The first Monday in April is unlucky because Cain was born on that Monday and Abel died on a Monday.
- The second Monday in August is the anniversary of the destruction of Sodom and Gomorrah.
- The last Monday in December is when Judas betrayed Jesus.

It is not clear how anyone knew these three things about Monday.

Tuesday If the first person you meet on Tuesday morning is left-handed, the encounter will bring you bad luck.

Wednesday A good day all round. Good for business meetings, medical treatment and writing important letters.

Thursday Variable. For some, a day of brave behaviour, and forward-looking ideas. But there's a proviso: Henry VIII's children, Edward VI, Mary Tudor and Elizabeth I, all died on a Thursday, thus developing a counter-superstition that Thursday can be very unlucky.

Friday For Christians, those who believe Jesus died on Friday hold to the superstition that Friday is therefore not a good day. For some, this is reinforced by the imaginative belief that Adam and Eve were expelled from the Garden of Eden on a Friday. But the good news is that, according to an old superstition, if you dream on Friday night and tell someone about it on Saturday, your dream will come true.

Saturday A dangerous day of restrictions and ill health, except for Jewish people who hold the Sabbath on Saturday. Bad luck follows those who leave hospital on a Saturday, and if a new moon appears on any Saturday, it will be followed by bad luck and rainy weather. The good news is that anyone born on a Saturday will have the gift of being able to see ghosts!

Sunday Christians see it as the most fortunate day. But more generally, if new clothes are kept until Sunday, then worn for the first time on that day, they will last twice as long. There is also one rather chilling warning: cutting fingernails on a Sunday brings very bad luck.

deafness

An old Scottish superstition regarding deafness is that a mixture of ant eggs and onion juice will ease the condition. In England, by contrast, you mash up a snail and let its juice drip into the afflicted area. Then there are those who sideline ant eggs, onion juice and snails, and head out to catch an eel. Apparently oil from a cooked eel will remedy deafness. But easiest of all: simply make eardrops from ordinary urine.

See also **oysters**.

dice

Superstitions have naturally arisen around the throwing of dice. How do you persuade them to roll to your advantage?
- Blow on them. Why? It's an old-time superstition, possibly linked to the suspicion that unscrupulous gamers might coat one side of the dice with a kind of glue activated by being

blown on, making it stick to the surface so the upper number will be predictable.

◉ Before the toss, rub the dice on a red-headed person. Why? Who would know — it's a superstition!

dimples

Take your pick between:

Dimple in chin — devil within.

or

A dimple is where the angel's finger turned the sleeping face up to kiss it.

dogs

The family dog may be unaware of it, but it is associated with several superstitions. It is not uncommon to see a dog, supposedly contentedly alone, go into a slight bristle, prick its ears, emit an occasional low growl, and gaze intently — apparently at nothing. Ah, but the dog isn't alone! The ancients will tell you that dogs can see ghosts, spirits, fairies and even the Angel of Death.

Furthermore if a dog starts to whine and continues to do so for no apparent reason, it is foretelling a misfortune which is soon to occur. But if on the way to a business meeting, a black and white dog crosses your path, this indicates either (a) good luck at the meeting, or (b) disappointment and a poor outcome. Take your pick: it depends on which superstition you endorse.

But the dog can, quite painlessly, contribute to family health. If an illness befalls someone, the superstitious will take a few hairs from the ill person, put them between two slices of bread and feed the sandwich to the dog. When the dog has eaten it, the illness is transferred from the patient into the luckless dog!

Incidentally, the origin of a dog's cold nose is given a mythical origin in one of those stories often classified as 'biblical', though they're not in the Bible. This one has become attached to the Jewish account of Noah and the ark from the book of Genesis. The story has it that during the long time the animals spent in the ark, a dog one day discovered a leak and immediately pushed his nose into the aperture in order to stem the flow of water into the ark, which would have flooded all aboard. By the time he was discovered and the leak attended to, his nose was very cold — and all dogs since have had cold noses. It's a charming story — but you won't actually find it in the Bible.

An American proverb warns: Beware of the man who does not talk, and the dog who does not bark.

See also **worms**.

drunkenness

Over time, a number of preventions and cures have accumulated to deal with this common problem. However, there is sparse information about their effectiveness. Consider the following:
- Avoid the condition in advance by preparing and eating roast pig lungs.
- In the absence of any available pigs, slip an owl's egg into the drink of someone who is already drunk. If this is not available, some drops of the drinker's own blood or powder ground from the bones of a dead man will do — or one or two live eels.

If the above treatments are ineffective, it may become necessary to roll the drunkard in manure, force him to drink olive oil — then wrap his private parts in cloth soaked with vinegar.

See also **ivy**.

ears

Several superstitions pronounce judgement on a person's
character by the shape of their ears. If the ears are small, their
owner is miserly and mean, while big ears obviously indicate
generosity of spirit. Ears flat against the skull signify their owner
is a crude person lacking in refinement. Long ears show that the
owner is well endowed with wisdom. More puzzlingly, square-
shaped ears indicate a noble heart.

earrings

Nobody knows why, but superstition dictates that by piercing the
ears to hold earrings a person's eyesight will improve. Screw-on
earrings are believed to have no effect (surprise!).

Easter

Like Christmas, Easter celebrations are a sincere celebration
of major importance to Christianity, and include some customs
which have been gently absorbed from earlier superstitions.

Before Christianity, however, ancient celebrations were held in
praise of Eostra, the goddess of spring. As part of the festivities,
devotees of Eostra gave presents of decorated real eggs (long

before marshmallow-filled chocolate ones) as a reminder that spring inaugurates a renewal and continuation of life. This tradition was gradually grafted onto the more recent Christian Easter, re-interpreted slightly as signifying one *specific* new life. The 'spring' aspect of the festival's origins is entirely inappropriate in the southern hemisphere where Easter is in autumn, but the mock eggs and the imagery of new life have been absorbed as a custom accompanying the celebration.

Some superstitions which in earlier times became attached to the significance of Easter have largely faded away. It is rare to see even the most devoutly superstitious waiting up until dawn on Easter Day with a darkened glass in order to 'watch the sun dance'. Saving three new garments to wear for the first time on Easter Sunday was believed to bring you good fortune for the following year, but over centuries that superstition narrowed down to just wearing an Easter bonnet, and now little is heard even of that — except in song.

Rituals, customs and superstitions involving the moon are now dismissed rather loftily by Christianity as 'pagan' — though curiously the date for the Christian observation of Easter comes to our calendar each year by the oldest pagan date-fixing method of all — the position of the moon.

eggs

Eggs are fragile in any context — urban or rural. An ancient English rhyme provides both gloom and minor comfort:

Break an egg, break a leg;
Break two, your love is true;
Break three, woe to thee.

Of course, to eat a boiled egg you have to break it — but superstition advises that after consuming the egg be sure to break the shell with firm pokes of the spoon, because witches collect empty eggshells and use them to make magic to harm men at sea.

If you are served a double-yolker, two superstitions apply:
(a) the double-yolker is a sign of good luck coming your way;
(b) it is a warning that death will strike someone near you.

Another superstition decrees that eggs must not be brought in or taken out of the household after sunset. Also, it is unlucky to dream of eggs. But one after-sunset superstition has a practical purpose: if a child is having difficulty overcoming bed-wetting, add some finely ground-up eggshells to the child's milk for drinking.

elbow

An ancient superstition warns against kissing your own elbow — for if you do, your gender will change immediately. Such an occurrence would be rare, since kissing one's elbow seems impossible (though one or two people can actually do it).

engagement

More superstition surrounds the breaking of an engagement than the launching of it. If during the engagement period a woman decides she does not want to go through with it after all, she need not speak a word. Superstition advises that she just offer her fiancé the gift of a knife — and hope he will get the message that their relationship is being severed. But either party must take care to become engaged to someone else only one more time, for the devil waits to claim the soul of anyone with two unsuccessful engagements who enters a third one.

But for actually becoming engaged, there is a concept in America about omens attached to the actual day the proposal/engagement occurs:

Monday: the couple's life together will be busy and eventful.

Tuesday: a peaceful and harmonious union is predicted.

eyes

Long the focus of interpretation and misinterpretation, the eyes — their colour, shape and distance apart — have been assigned various superstitious qualities. An old American rhyme from Wyoming asserts:

> *Blue-eyed beauty — do your mammy's duty;*
> *Black eye — pick-a-pie, runaround and tell a lie;*
> *Grey eye — greedy gut, eat all the world up.*

But whatever their colour — if the left eye itches, there's bad luck afoot. However, if the right eye twitches, things are going to improve in your world.

If one of those eye infections known as a sty occurs, rub it gently with a wedding ring. If that seems too simple, some believe that bathing the eye in cow urine is more effective — or applying a mash of green garlic. Another way of curing a sty is to hold a cat's tail up against it and draw it slowly across the offending area (this requires a very co-operative cat).

In rather more serious vein, should an eye be diagnosed as having grown a cataract, this was believed curable by securing the head of a cat (just the head), burning it but saving all the ashes — then blowing them into the affected eye(s). Understandably, this was believed before medical science advanced to ophthalmology.

Wednesday: a partnership of constant agreement, without quarrels.

Thursday: future ambitions and wishes will be met.

Friday: rewards will come eventually, after much effort and some tribulation.

Saturday: the union will enjoy notable pleasures.

But once the proposal has been made and the couple enter the period of engagement, there are some superstitious restrictions which come into play:

- Until they are married, an engaged couple should not agree to be godparents to anyone's child, as it will place their own marriage in jeopardy.
- An engaged couple should not be photographed together. This dates back to the ancient concept, long before the advent of photography, that any picture of a person contained part of their life force, by which an evil spirit could gain influence on their soul — in this case, the success or not of the couple's union.

feet

Bernard Bresslau's 1959 hit song assured everyone that we need feet — 'to keep your sox on, and stop your legs from fraying at the ends.' But we are assured from other quarters that we need them for additional things, and there are superstitions to tell us:

⊚ To start any new journey, lead with the right foot, not the left.
⊚ Do not enter a house with your left foot first — particularly a bride coming to her first home.
⊚ When dressing, put the right shoe on first (if the left one is put on first, the day will go badly).

Feet with high insteps attract two interpretations from the superstitious. The Chinese would have it that people with a high foot arch are independent and self-sufficient. But Britain and America tend to the superstition that a high instep indicates good breeding (parts of the United States further observe that foot arches high enough to let water flow through demonstrate the finest ancestry).

According to the old beliefs:

⊚ A person with short fat fingers must be dim-witted.
⊚ If forefinger and thumb cannot meet around the opposite wrist, that person is a glutton.
⊚ Long fingers may well indicate an inherent artistic temperament.

- But long fingers can also indicate an inability to be prudent with money.
- If just the middle finger is longer than the forefinger, that person cannot be trusted.
- Anyone born with an extra finger will have lifelong good luck.
- A person born with a permanently bent finger will have an unpleasant temper.
- The right-hand forefinger should never be used to put ointment on any damage — it is called the Poison Finger.
- If two people speak the same word at the same time, they must lock their little fingers together (left to left, right to right), make a silent wish, then say nothing more until the fingers are released.

See also **wedding ring**.

fingernails

Should white spots be seen growing in your nails, then at some point before the spots reach the end and are cut off you'll have some good luck. If a spot appears on the thumbnail, an unexpected gift is heading your way. But if black spots occur on the nail, then bad luck is on the way.

There are also severe superstitious rules about the cutting of fingernails:

Cut them on Monday, cut them for health;
Cut them on Tuesday, cut them for wealth;
Cut them on Wednesday, cut them for news;
Cut them on Thursday, a new pair of shoes;
Cut them on Friday, cut them for sorrow;
Cut them on Saturday, true love tomorrow;
Cut them on Sunday, the devil will come
And stay all the week till his evil is done.

See also **fingers**.

fingers

Believers in superstitions can use their 'knowledge' to make judgements on the characters of other people — just by looking at their fingers.

flowers

Through no fault of their own, white flowers arouse gloomy superstitions. To take some into a room is courting disaster, especially if they have nodding heads like snowdrops or if they are sweet-scented varieties — for that scent is the souls of the departed dead. And if asleep and dreaming you have a vision of white flowers, the death in question is going to be someone close to you. On the other hand, red blossoms are all right, since red blooms are the colour of blood and therefore symbolise life. But if you are taking or sending flowers to a hospital patient, do not mix red blooms with white. There is a superstition that a red-and-white bouquet signals that there will soon be a death on the ward.

four

In some oriental cultures — namely Korean, Chinese and Japanese — fear and superstition surround the number four. This stems from the fact that the word for 'four' in their languages sounds very similar to the word for 'death'. Mentioning the number 4 around a sick relative is strongly avoided. Numbering for houses, floors of high-rise buildings, wards in hospitals, tables in restaurants, military aircraft and shipping all avoid 4 whenever possible, and 3A is frequently used in its place. For some, 4 April — the fourth day of the fourth month — is considered unlucky, and the ultra-conservative also avoid figures such as 14, 24 and 43 because they include the undesirable number 4.

four-leafed clover

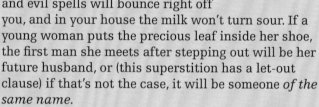

A four-leafed clover has superstition going into a spin. Find one, and you'll be able to see fairies and recognise evil spirits, which will give you the ability to tell who is secretly a witch. Carry it with you and evil spells will bounce right off you, and in your house the milk won't turn sour. If a young woman puts the precious leaf inside her shoe, the first man she meets after stepping out will be her future husband, or (this superstition has a let-out clause) if that's not the case, it will be someone *of the same name.*

It has been estimated that in nature, there may be one four-leaf among approximately 10,000 three-leaf clovers. When found, each of the four leaves has a duty to fulfil: the first is for faith, the second is for hope, the third is for love, and the fourth is for luck. Note: It is perhaps worth adding that in recent years horticulturalists have successfully developed a clover plant with four leaves exclusively, so the purchase of a 'four-leaf-clover kit set' will enable you to grow as many as you like.

Friday

Some people feel a foreboding about Friday arising from various superstitions, which appear to be based on traditional events (but events with no very firm provenance).

For instance, it is often said that 'Jesus was killed on a Friday'.

Being a tradition doesn't make this a fact. There is some eyebrow-raising about whether the week in its current form was acknowledged in AD 33, and even if it were, the discovery of the southern hemisphere and the invention of time zones make it difficult in many places to identify what time it is in Israel and even what day.

The more inventive of our forefathers said that Eve offered Adam the 'apple' (the Bible just says 'fruit') on a Friday, and that Cain slew Abel on a Friday. Even more surprising is the belief that Noah's ark set sail on a Friday. How these events from thousands of years ago came to be attached to a specific weekday nobody knows, but the bad vibes linger.

And there's more. Witches meet in covens for a strategy meeting every Friday. And the 'Friday is bad' superstition comes down hard on children's birth (a matter over which no one normally has any control), namely: children born on a Friday will have unlucky lives, but will be recompensed by being psychic and with the ability to heal others.

See also **Black Friday**; **thirteen**.

garlic

As far back as Ancient Egypt, garlic has been credited as a protection against a wide range of problems — and not just for its notable flavour.

At least two versions of its origin ignore that it is just a plant, *allium sativum*, a tasty and aromatic member of the onion family. Early Egyptians perceived garlic as a gift from the gods, but post-biblical mythology decreed that it grew where Satan's left foot trod as he was evicted from the Garden of Eden (the print of his right foot gave rise to ordinary onions).

Superstition has long credited garlic with various powers: protecting sailors from storms and shipwreck; giving soldiers courage; protecting miners from evil underground demons; if placed under the pillows of babies, protecting them overnight; and as household garlands to protect against illness, witches, robbers and vampires.

The perceived connection between vampires and garlic was slow in reaching the English language. The first vampire story in English, *The Vampyre* by John Polidori (1819), makes no mention of garlic. Irish author Bram Stoker's later vampire novel, *Dracula* (1897), introduced the powerful effects between vampires and what they greatly fear: daylight — and garlic. But as a protection it had been widely used long before that — against toothache, sunstroke, leprosy, even bed-wetting.

Medical research can identify a genuine physical condition called alliumphobia — a powerful dislike, even fear of garlic. And there is a medical theory that some people simply must not eat garlic because it causes disorder in certain blood types. Scholars point out that this condition, and its necessary repudiation of anything to do with garlic, may be a contributing factor to the legend of vampires and their avoidance of garlic.

The vampire legends were believed historically in southern Slavic countries and Romania, where an eye was kept on those who refused to eat garlic. Consequently, superstition decreed that cloves of garlic be placed in the mouths of the deceased before they were buried, to ward off any passing vampire.

goat

The goat has long been associated with the Devil or Satan, who can often be seen in artwork with a goat's cloven hooves, and sometimes with a goat's head. Superstitious folk believed that real goats are genuinely in association with the Devil. The belief goes a giant step further — by reporting that when a goat needs its 'beard' combed, the goat visits the Devil in person, who will attend to it.

But a more amiable superstition about the goat is quite user-friendly: if a goat's horn is kept under the pillow, it will cure insomnia.

gold

In ancient interpretations of precious metals, gold signified the sun and silver the moon. Qualities associated with gold differed according to the culture, but included incorruptibility, the power of resurrection and/or immortality, and the ability to fly (if you were a god). Not committing itself to any of these, the Bible nevertheless acknowledges the 'preciousness' of gold; by one count, gold is mentioned 400 times in scripture.

The modern concept of gold focuses on its primary attributes: that it is precious and beautiful. But shadows of two old superstitions still lurk:
- Infection in and around the eye can be cured by stroking the affected area with gold — preferably a wedding ring.
- At the point where a rainbow meets the earth, there will be a pot of gold. Every television news crew in the world is waiting for someone to find it — nobody has yet.

See also **eyes; rainbows**.

Good Friday

One of the strangest post-crucifixion superstitions is that Christians should not do any laundry on Good Friday, because the garments will never wash truly clean. Why? Legend has it that while Jesus was being taken away to be crucified, he was slapped in the face by a wet garment and dirty laundry water, so he issued a curse that no such washing should ever be done again on that day.

There are other Good Friday superstitions:
- Because of the role which nails played in the death of Jesus, blacksmiths and carpenters should not work with them on this day.
- Children should be discouraged from climbing trees on Good Friday, because Jesus died on wood.

But in more optimistic vein:
- Good Friday is a good day for going fishing — and for weaning babies.
- If a hot cross bun is kept from one Good Friday until the next, the house will be protected from damage and fires.

⊚ Good Friday is a favourable day to cure a wart. To begin the process, stop speaking. Then cut a potato in half, rub the cut surfaces over the wart, feed the potato pieces to a cow, and remain silent until the cow has finished eating the potato. The wart will then disappear.

See also **Black Friday**.

gooseberry bush

Curious children ask, 'Where do babies come from?' A traditional 'olde-tyme' response is that babies are found 'under a gooseberry bush'. The only known origin for this answer is less than decorous, since babies *do* actually come from what is sometimes referred to as . . . a 'bush'.

gremlins

Gremlins are mischievous supernatural creatures with a particular love of messing up machinery and mechanical structures. Gremlins came to public recognition more recently than other supernatural creatures. According to some sources, they were first mentioned in World War One, and the word was in general use among Royal Air Force personnel by the 1920s. An early appearance of the gremlin in print came from aviatrix and Air Force Commandant Pauline Gower, who, in the Air Transport Auxiliary's magazine in 1938, described Scotland as 'gremlin country' — where pilots must be on the alert for mischief caused by destructive interference.

Awareness of gremlins (or rather the mishaps caused by them) grew among airmen in World War Two, and former pilot (and later famous children's author) Roald Dahl published a book in 1943 entitled *The Gremlins*. The term then gradually gained wider currency and was no longer restricted to aircraft problems. Even the non-superstitious choose to suspend disbelief when something goes annoyingly wrong, and blame it on 'gremlins'.

The word gremlin itself is of unclear origin. It may be a version of the Irish word *gruaimin* (an evil-tempered man), or borrowed from the Danish *græmling* (an imp), or descended from an old English word *gremian* (to anger). However, the most likely explanation is that it is a combination of the surname of the Brothers Grimm (indicating a connection to the supernatural) with the second half of Fremlin's — a widely known British brewery whose beer was stocked in the RAF bar when the word began to circulate. But the precise origin of the word has never been found. The gremlins got at it.

hair

Ancient superstition decrees that a person's hair contains their 'essential spirit' (this could be a forerunner of what we now call DNA). Therefore, anyone who has a strand or lock of your hair has the power to command your person and bewitch you. So should you give such a valuable key to your life and soul to another person, personal love and deep trust are involved. Accordingly, parents who keep a lock of their child's hair into the child's adulthood must guard it with extreme care, lest it be damaged, or worse, stolen. The child's essential spirit could be in danger from a stranger with evil intent.

Male hair is often perceived to be associated with strength. The obvious example is Samson the Israelite, but there are also many jokes about hairy-chested men (and a relevant superstition foretells that men with hairy arms have a future of great riches). Hair colour sometimes unfairly pigeonholes the owner's personality:

>   red: fiery and energetic;
>   dark (brown or black): brave, reliable, often successful;
>   fair: possibly shy, timid;
>   grey: wise.

Of course, the availability of mass-produced hair dyes has rather upset these assessments. (A survey reported that Americans spent $1.6 billion annually on hair colouring in order *not* to show grey.) A curious supposition that Judas Iscariot, the betrayer of Jesus, had red hair nurtured the unfounded suspicion of red-haired people. Even Shakespeare makes the connection, when, in *As You Like It*, Rosalind says of Orlando:

His hair is of the dissembling colour . . .
and Celia replies:
It is something browner than Judas's . . .

The redhead (ginger, copper, auburn) is subject to other ancient and very dubious judgements:
- a fiery temper;
- an ardent lover;
- possibly an unfaithful husband;
- cruel by nature — if the beard is also red;
- and (somewhat unexpectedly) hopeless at churning butter!

Anyone nervous of ephemeral evil creatures must meticulously collect all clippings after a haircut and burn them. Leaving them lying about is an open invitation to witches, interfering spirits — and birds. The witches, now having part of your body, will cast spells to cause you harm. And passing birds could pick up some of your clippings and weave them into their nest, thus causing you to suffer debilitating headaches.

Halloween

While bread and circuses now surround Christmas and Easter, they have not entirely obliterated the universal awareness of the Christian reason for the importance of these two occasions. Halloween, on the other hand, has become an entirely commercial event, with popular observance of its ancient superstitions as 'customs'. There is little or no general awareness of the reason for its existence.

After the Christian religion developed the concept of celebrating saints, All Hallows Day was allocated to the start of the northern winter: 1 November ('Hallows' as in 'very holy', thus saints), so the night before, 31 October, became known as All Hallows Evening — eventually modified to Halloween.

The original ancient superstitious concept was that on one occasion each year, before all the saints were celebrated, on All Hallows Evening the veil between the living and the dead would be lifted. The dead would be allowed to roam the earth, either invisibly or as visible ghosts. If they had been evil and macabre when alive, then they could be seen like that again for just that one night.

Over time, Halloween gathered dozens of superstitions, some offering words of warning:
- To keep evil spirits away, walk three times backwards around your home before the sun sets.
- On Halloween night do not turn round if you hear footsteps behind you.
- If moonlight throws shadows, do not look at your own.
- Stand in the middle of a crossroad and listen to the wind — it will tell your future.
- If you see a spider, do not kill it. It could be the soul of a dead person from your own family.
- If you eat a salted herring before going to bed, your future lover will come to you in a dream.
- Spend the evening with your pockets turned inside out and no evil spirit will accost you.
- A baby born on Halloween is completely protected from evil spirits.
- At Halloween make a dish of mashed potatoes and hide a ring in it. When the potatoes are served, the person who gets the ring will be first of the group to marry.

The majority of such superstitions have faded from use, while the others have been gently revised as seldom-questioned 'customs'. For example:

- Dressing in evil costumes. This satisfies the superstition that it is best not to be recognised on Halloween, because a returning dead soul with a grudge may be seeking you out. Others dress in costumes reflecting the 'visitors' from beyond the veil who are not normally seen: witches, warlocks, corpses, devils and supernatural personalities. Again, such disguises protect the wearer from evil.

- In early centuries in England, Scotland and Ireland, a Halloween practice was to take a hollowed-out turnip and cut holes in the front as a crude form of face, then place a lighted candle inside. Its purpose was to frighten away spirits visiting from the dead, so it was either placed in a house window to show there was already a 'spirit' in residence, or carried along the roads at night when out and about — again to alert any passing ghoul to keep away. Scots and Irish who emigrated to the new country America took their Halloween practices with them, but turnips were not easily available, so the immigrants scouted around and found pumpkins. Readily available and easily carved, the pumpkin virtually took over the Halloween celebration in America, and is ubiquitous in image and reality right through October. It appears in some unexpected guises, such as 'gourmet Halloween Chocolates — pumpkin filled'.

- From early centuries the festival included 'guising', 'mumming' and 'souling'. Citizens dressed in the bizarre horror costumes customary for the occasion (guising), then performed simple dances or songs (mumming) for wealthier folk, and in return for some sweetmeats or a cake, promised to pray for their dead relatives (souling). Suggestions might tentatively be made that some minor mischief might occur if they were turned away. Shakespeare mentions it in *The Two Gentlemen of Verona*:

    to speak puling, like a beggar at Hallowmas.
    (puling = moaning, as in a drawn-out, anxious cry)

By the 1920s, the old customs of guising, mumming and souling, introduced by immigrants into America, had melded into 'trick or treat', which became a major part of the Halloween evening.

hand

It is totally unfair to people born left-handed, but ancient superstitions are firm that the right hand belongs to God and the left hand belongs to the Devil, who also lives part of his time over your left shoulder. Several biblical references acknowledge the right side as the place of honour: '. . . and sat at the right hand of God' (Mark 16:19); 'Sit at my right hand . . .' (Matthew 22:44). The Bible condemns 'aliens, whose mouths speak lies, and whose right hand is a right hand of falsehood' (Psalm 144:8), indicating that the norm in biblical times would have been the right hand affirming the truth, not falsehood.

The custom of swearing a formal or legal oath with the right hand raised is common, though not universal. The 'right hand' superstition seems also to have influenced the American pledge of allegiance, when the right hand is placed over the heart.

At a less formal level, superstition tells us that if the palm of the right hand itches, money is coming to you. If the palm of the left hand itches, you have to pay out some money.

See also **shaking hands**.

hats

Superstitions about hats were once numerous, but have not had a good survival rate. Nearly all of them have faded — possibly from a slow death of belief in their predictions, since none seemed to come true. For instance, an old superstition warns that putting a hat on back-to-front will result in bad luck for the rest of the day. This does not seem to have affected the large proportion of 21st century youth who prefer to wear their baseball caps peaked at the back, instead of the intended front.

The old belief that men on the street must take their hats off to acknowledge a passing woman acquaintance has also faded. Similarly, men do not always remove their hats when a funeral goes past today. Superstition warns that failure to do so means that the next death will be their own. Disaster doesn't seem to have struck men not observing either of these 'courtesies' — if in fact they were even wearing a hat.

Another rather limiting superstition predicts dire consequences if a hat is ever put down on a table or a bed, or worse — *under* a bed. Very bad luck will follow. But there is an 'out clause': buy a new hat as soon as possible and the bad luck will waft away. If hats are worn inside a building, the wearer will get a headache. This superstition is difficult to take seriously, and it's surprising that it ever was, particularly as some organisations, ranks and religions actually require head covering, even indoors.

Religions have spawned contrasting beliefs around the wearing of hats. For Sikhs, the wearing of a turban at all times is a vital article of faith (though it is not regarded as a 'hat'). Jewish men must wear a head covering during any religious service, but Christian men (other than prelates of church authority) are expected to be bare-headed. Curiously, the Christian men-no-hats border is crossed at high level with a tradition borrowed from the synagogue by the Pope, who customarily wears a Jewish yarmulke or skull cap.

Various kinds of hats have long held significance in denoting levels of rank, either social, professional or administrative. Some still do (the military, royalty, religious orders), but the wearing of hats and their significance have both sharply declined.

A study by Professor Andrew Gurr, *Shakespeare's Hats*, reveals the enormously complex rules surrounding the wearing of hats in the centuries Shakespeare depicts. For example, in the presence of a king it is ingrained that everyone must take their hat off (with their right hand — thus less likely to suddenly use a weapon). So when Shakespeare's Richard II believes he has been 'un-kinged', he tells his followers to 'cover your heads'. As he is no longer a king, he cannot expect them to bare their heads.

Also, when Hamlet decides to 'put an antic disposition on', a distraught Ophelia describes him:

> *with his doublet all unbrac'd, no hat upon his head, his stockings fouled.*

She is accustomed to seeing him always with some kind of head covering. To be without it is 'antic' indeed.

One fatality of the decline in hats has been a word once very frequently seen: hatter. Both making and selling them are now, alas, very rare.

hawthorn

Hawthorn is not frequently found in urban areas, being strictly a rural product. But superstition warns anyone tempted to bring its blossom into the house, because death comes with it. The origin of this cheerful prediction is from those who believe that hawthorn formed the crown of thorns on Jesus' head during the crucifixion.

Alas, the issue of which thorns crowned Jesus is fraught, because there are several claimants. Besides hawthorn, the infamous crown is also said to have been made from the jujuba tree; the Jerusalem locust tree; the bramble rose; and the popular garden plant *euphorbia millii*, conveniently known as the 'crown of thorns', though named long after the biblical event.

Fortunately, another superstition dismisses hawthorn's ominous image and welcomes it into the house, because it will protect the family, particularly any new baby. Furthermore, the pro-hawthorners believe the gentle perfume of hawthorn blossom is an aid to romantic encounters.

headache

An optimistic cure involves wrapping the head tightly in the skin of a snake. If that isn't easily obtainable, then an alternative cure is to wind a hangman's rope around the head (though this could possibly be harder to locate than a snakeskin). Without a convenient snake or co-operative hangman, a third alternative is to tie the head of a dead buzzard onto the forehead. In the absence of a snakeskin, hangman's rope or dead buzzard, a further recommendation is to scrape some moss from the inside of a formerly buried human skull and sniff it. As a last resort — and perhaps this will be easier to find — apply a poultice made from cow dung to the aching head.

Then there is willow bark. The use of willow bark to relieve pain dates back thousands of years to the time of Hippocrates (400 BC), when patients were advised to chew on the bark to reduce fever and inflammation. It was also a known remedy for centuries in China and parts of Europe. The bark of white willow contains salicin (a chemical similar to acetylsalicylic acid). In combination with the willow's powerful anti-inflammatory plant compounds (called flavonoids), salicin is thought to be responsible for the genuine pain-relieving and anti-inflammatory effects of the herb. During the 1800s, salicin was used to develop aspirin, and continues to be used today for the treatment of pain (particularly lower back pain and osteoarthritis) and inflammatory conditions, such as bursitis, tendinitis — and headaches.

The ancients got that one right.

hearse
While at a family funeral, those who are superstitious may feel a tremor if the hearse carrying their loved one has to reverse or turn around for any reason. This is a sure way of offending the corpse — and causing the death of another family member quite soon.

heartburn
In the absence of modern pharmaceuticals for heartburn, indigestion or acid reflux, ancient folk remedies were available. One such was sucking a lump of coal; while for the brave, chewing on some ground-up toenails was recommended.

hellebores
A suburban garden with a drift of green-and-white hellebores may have a value the gardener didn't realise. There are various superstitions:
⊛ White hellebore blooms can cure madness, leprosy and rabies.
⊛ If not needed for those emergencies, hellebore blooms, regularly fed to children before breakfast, will promote intelligence and mental health.

herrings (salted)
When suffering from a sore throat, an old superstition decrees it can be relieved by placing a salted herring on the feet of the afflicted.

holly

Deck the halls with boughs of it — why? For several thousand years before Jesus and the celebrations around his birth evolved, halls were being decked with holly. Druids, Celts and ancient Romans were impressed with its hardy ability to stay green throughout the most bitter of winters, and brought boughs of it indoors to remind them that green would return to the world, come spring.

So the green holly represented the continuity of life. But more importantly, the harshness of the foliage and its unpleasant thorns were believed to repel witches or demons who might have fancied visiting the household and causing trouble. A sprig of holly was retained in the house for the rest of the year; a comforting superstition ruled that this sprig would protect the house from lightning.

Another superstition was reserved for young women. To predict her future, she should pull the prickles off a random leaf one by one, reciting 'girl, wife, widow, nun'. When she reached the last prickle, her future would be revealed.

Much later, as Christianity developed, those powers of preventing trouble became useful to new Christians, who placed holly on their doors to prevent possible persecution. But as Christianity grew, elements of the holly began to be absorbed into a set of new traditions. Its prickly foliage came to be a reminder of the crown of thorns worn by Jesus during the crucifixion, with its brilliant red berries representing drops of his blood.

Holly moved into mainstream acceptance as part of the festival of Christmas and became one of its festive elements, so much so that the early symbolism of winter stability, then pain from the thorn crown and blood caused by thorns were eased aside. Holly blossomed into cheery Christmas cards, sat atop puddings (sometimes with plastic berries in warmer climates) and adorned electrically lit twinkling door wreaths.

In its comparatively recent association with a major Christian festival, holly gained some new legends.

1. In one story, an orphaned boy came to the manger where baby Jesus lay and put down a bunch of holly as a gift, then cried — because he was only able to give something so humble. Baby Jesus saw his sorrow and touched the gift where the teardrops fell — which all turned into beautiful red berries. (Note: Alas, holly had red berries for several millennia before Jesus was born.)

2. During the wrath of King Herod, the holly grew extra branches and leaves to help hide the holy family.

3. Designating the wood from which the crucifixion cross was made has generated at least ten legends. It is said to have been made from: cedar; dogwood; poplar; pine; mistletoe; cypress; olive; aspen; elder — and holly.

honeymoon

The origin of the custom, and its name, are clouded with layers of mystery. One belief is that in some ancient cultures a man seeking a particular woman as a wife simply abducted her and took her away into hiding for a month while she got used to the idea, then they returned to their normal life, but now as a couple. While this (curiously) rules out any of the customs surrounding a wedding ceremony, since there wasn't one, it could be the progenitor of the superstitions surrounding the veil, the bridesmaids and the groomsmen, namely their duty of protection from anyone plotting to abduct the bride.

The word 'honeymoon' has mild superstitious overtones, in that honey has long been regarded as a sweet helper to love (a gentle aid to fertility and sex — rather than the formal term 'aphrodisiac'). But over centuries no superstition became responsible for the custom which seemed to grow that after either the wedding or the abduction, the couple ate honey and drank mead for 30 days — a full cycle of the moon. Hence 'honey-moon'.

hops

Besides being a popular ingredient of beer, hops have one other favourable use: a bunch hung in the house helps keep the good luck coming.

horse

Even horses have attracted superstitions:

- It is bad luck to meet a white horse. If you see one, you must spit and make a wish.
- Even if a horse has only white feet, it is still unlucky.

Alternatively:

- It is good luck to meet a white horse.
- A horse with only white feet is also lucky.

As long as 5000 years ago, when people still believed that witches flew the world at night, horse owners created anti-witch devices to fend off the evil ones using their horses for night-time rides. Known to us as 'horse-brasses', they were decorative and ornamental and always kept very shiny, in order to dazzle any evil being who came too close.

To the superstitious, several optimistic ways of curing human medical problems are made possible by a horse — or its collar. Old-time Pennsylvanians treated a child's colic by passing the child three times through a horse collar — which must still be warm after being removed from a horse. If the child's sickness developed further, the next stage in the cure was to pass the child three times under the horse's belly and out the other side.

In 1747 Methodist theologian John Wesley published *Primitive Physick*, which included a slightly unexpected remedy for breast cancer, using the calluses found inside horses' legs:

Take horse spurs from the inside of horses' fore-legs and dry them by the fire till they will beat to powder. Sift and

infuse two drachms in two quarts of ale; drink half a pint
every six hours with new warm milk. It has cured many.
(drachm = 3.5 grams or .12 of an ounce)

horseshoe

Horseshoes in one form or another existed in ancient Greece and
have long been associated with good luck, though it's not clear
why. They were traditionally made from iron, which for many
centuries was considered a 'magical' metal. Also, the horseshoe's
traditional crescent shape is reminiscent of a crescent
moon's shape. Taken together, these factors contributed to the
development through the centuries of a range of superstitions.

One of these is that finding a cast-off horseshoe brings the best
level of luck, especially if the finder spits on it, tosses it over the
left shoulder, then picks it up and takes it home to nail above
a doorway. From that point on, dispute exists over whether it
should hang up or down.

Version 1: *Up* — and the luck is retained in the house where the
shoe hangs.
Down — and the luck will slowly drip away.

Version 2: *Up* — and the luck is retained inside the horseshoe
and does the house little good.
Down — and the luck will be cast more easily on those
beneath.

Either way, if any witches are about they won't come near
when they see a horseshoe. And the fact that horseshoes were
commonly held in place by *seven* nails was a further addition to
its image of good luck.

A marvellously fantastic story introduced the horseshoe magic
into Christianity, maintaining the ancient 'protection' quality
of the horseshoe and the aura of luck around it. The legend

maintains that Britain's St Dunstan (a onetime blacksmith who later became Archbishop of Canterbury in AD 959) once dealt with a customer who wanted his own feet shod! Noting that the aforementioned feet were cloven, Dunstan recognised that the client was Satan himself, so he explained that to do the job he must tie the customer to the wall. This was done, and Dunstan proceeded to perform the most painful treatment he could summon on the cloven feet of the customer, who begged for mercy. Blacksmith Dunstan promised relief *only* if the client gave a solemn promise never to enter a house which had a horseshoe above the door.

Among the many who believed in the protective qualities of the horseshoe was Lord Nelson, who had one nailed to the mast of the *Victory*. It may have helped in the victory over Britain's enemies, even if it was not much help to Nelson himself.

Whether she consciously observes superstition or not, a bride often carries a mock version of a horseshoe, thus following a variation of an ancient 'luck' superstition. Hers is likely to be pleated white satin — not iron, as is the symbol's origin. Whether the horseshoe is attached to the ribbon upside-down or right-way-up has been a matter of contention for some centuries.

See also **U**.

hot cross buns

Long before their association with the Christian commemoration of Easter, sweet buns with their top divided into four were an ingredient of various festivals. Buns topped with a quartered surface were baked in cultures as diverse as the ancient Egyptian, Greek, Saxon, Chinese, Mexican and Peruvian. The usual focus was festivals celebrating spring, when the four divisions of the moon were marked on the bun's surface.

In the Bible, the book of Jeremiah refers to the ancient Jewish custom of offering 'sacred breads' to the queen of heaven — the moon.

Cultures which sometimes sacrificed an ox or bullock to the gods accompanied such occasions with festive buns, the surface of which featured one pair of oxen horns atop another pair upside down, thus making an X figure. Centuries later, during the growth of Christianity, the lines making the cross shape of two pairs of bullock horns and/or the four quarters of the moon came to be adapted into Christian imagery, referencing the cross on which Jesus died.

The term 'hot cross buns' first appeared in print in *Poor Robin's Almanack* (1733), and the new Christian version of the bun gathered several superstitions:

- A bun with a cross could be seen as a charm against evil, so one was frequently withheld from the Easter table and retained for good protection over the coming year. It would keep for that year without going mouldy or stale.
- A shaving from this kept bun, mixed with milk, would help someone recover from illness.
- Men of the sea carrying a crossed bun in their craft would be protected against shipwreck.
- Farmers would keep a bun where they stored their grain, as rats were believed to avoid them.

In all these cases, the buns were only effective *if baked on Good Friday*.

house

Whether you know it or not, a whole family of superstitions is waiting to move into your house — if some aren't already there. So if you are moving into a house which is new to you, the householder should walk through each room, carrying a loaf of bread and some salt. This will reassure any spirits already living in the place that the new inhabitants will not cause them trouble.

It will also help to fend off any evil spirits which may be lurking with intent to enter. From then on, the following preventative superstitions will help preserve the house from danger:

- Always ensure guests leave by the same door they entered (if they go out by any other door they are taking away some of the household luck).
- Guests of the newly installed occupants should be encouraged to bring gifts of coal and salt.
- Pets in the new home should have their paws smeared with butter, to distract them from roaming.
- And most importantly, to avoid household fire, locate the blouse of a virgin and bury it in the garden inside a jar.

hydrangeas

Seemingly the most innocent and down-home of garden flowers, the hydrangea carries an ancient superstition of special significance to any household with unmarried daughters. If the hydrangea grows too close to the house, especially near the doors, the daughters of the house will remain unmarried.

impotence

If they have faith in an old superstition, men who are concerned about their sexual vigour should eat a generous amount of rabbit kidneys. Rabbits are known to be very procreative, but why their kidneys were regarded as the seat of their rampant passions has never been explained. (Nor is there any suggestion that another part of the male rabbit might provide a more logical encouragement.)

There are alternative remedies based in superstition: celery boiled to a pulp and eaten hot; two cloves of garlic eaten every day (but the cumulative effect takes three months); fermented bamboo paste (presumably utilising the soft leafy parts of the plant). Other slightly easier options are oysters, avocados and dark chocolate! There is no medical evidence that any of those is effective, but Doron S. Stember, MD, a urologist at Beth Israel Medical Centre in New York, says in their defence:

If a man believes he responds to a particular aphrodisiac, then, by definition, it works for him — it may just be due to the placebo effect.

See also **olive oil**.

invisibility

Incredibly, superstitions do exist giving instructions on how to become invisible. There is little chance of anyone making themselves invisible by accident, because superstitions advising how to achieve that state make it clear that there must be detailed planning.

- While carrying a lump of agate, the aspiring invisible-ee must collect spores from a bracken fern (not easy: the spores are *very* small) and then collect the right eye of a bat. Place the mixture inside your shoe and walk about.
- If that doesn't work, a further step must be taken. Dig up a dead body, remove your own shirt and also the corpse's shirt, then change them over so that you are wearing the corpse's shirt.

iron

For countless centuries, iron has been regarded as a supernaturally potent metal — able to protect against bad luck and to send any approaching evil forces packing. Witches, for instance, cannot travel over iron — so scissors or a knife laid under your welcome mat at the door will persuade them to go somewhere else.

- To protect the baby, an iron poker laid over their cradle will keep them safe.
- When someone is sick, if a piece of iron is rested upon them, then taken outside and nailed to a tree, the illness will be transferred to the tree.
- Putting a (clean) piece of iron into your mouth the day before Easter and biting on it will keep toothache away for the remainder of the year.
- If you suffer from night-time cramps, and have the luck to know where an old and dusty sword can be obtained, keep it by your bedside and cramps will no longer bother you.

ivory

Ivory is an animal product and carries its own endowment of superstition: it is simply regarded as lucky. But it has a specific benefit too: if you carry ivory it will ward off cancer.

Ivory's progenitor, the elephant, carries a deal of symbolism along with its impressive bulk. In some cultures the elephant is venerated as a symbol of fertility, wisdom and royalty. The Hindu god of wisdom and success, Ganesh, is depicted with an elephant's head.

Because it is considered to be animal royalty itself, the elephant frequently carries royal persons and others of similarly elevated rank. And although royals probably didn't bother, any ordinary citizen who possesses a hair from the elephant's tail will have a run of good luck. But should you have an ornament or a picture of an elephant in your house, there is a belief that it should be facing the door — that way, happiness and prosperity will know to enter the house.

ivy

Ivy might be a heavy drinker's best friend. Find some ivy seeds and dissolve them in vinegar. Then take some leaves, boil them and keep the water. Before a night out, drink some of the vinegar mixture, and when the evening is over, drink some of the leaf-water.

kingfisher

Kingfisher birds are of royal descent. Their ultimate progenitor
was Alcyone, daughter of Aeolus, King of the Winds. Grief-
stricken at the death of her husband, who had been drowned
in a shipwreck, Alcyone threw herself into the sea, and the
sympathetic gods turned her and her husband into kingfishers.
Then the kingfisher legends and superstitions grew:

⊚ Kingfishers make their nests floating on the sea (they don't).
⊚ Named after their progenitor, 'halcyon days' are the seven days
  before and seven after the winter solstice.
⊚ Halcyon days occurred because Alcyone's royal father ordered
  the seas to be calm while the kingfishers' nests were floating on
  the sea (though they weren't).
⊚ Later on, the kingfisher was the first bird Noah sent out when
  the flood ended. It flew high and its back feathers gained the
  wonderful blue of the sky that day after the flood. (This story
  has no biblical foundation.)
⊚ Carrying a few of those same blue feathers with you acts as a
  charm ensuring good health and good luck.

Finally, in ancient times in one part of Russia the Ostiac people
believed that carrying a small bag containing the skin, bill and
claws of a (dead) kingfisher would provide freedom from fear.

kiss

A kiss has several distinct manifestations. It is perceived mainly as a gesture of physical affection, ranging from cuddling a new baby; farewelling a child going to school or on holiday; greeting your grandmother; congratulating a winner — and also, of course, being a stepping-stone to serious shared emotions. But a kiss can also be bestowed for quite different purposes on other recipients: a Bible, a hand, a papal ring, even a stone (as in Blarney — in itself a *major* superstition).

Apart from the well-known normal human interaction of kissing as part of physical passion, since time immemorial the act of a (fairly light) kiss has held a powerful superstitious image of conveying a range of other thoughts and wishes: some kinds of magic; humility; religious fervour; acceptance of authority; loyalty; plus, in the most ordinary of circumstances, the hope of luck. Participants in a match of skills sometimes bestow a quick kiss on a golf ball, a hand of cards, boxing gloves, a surf board, and frequently on betting slips and lottery tickets. And if victory is gained, quite often the trophy is kissed — triumphant sportsmen often do so after winning a cup.

But it isn't all good news:
- An affectionate kiss on someone's nose will lead to a disaster — probably a quarrel between the kisser and the kissee.
- Leaning over someone's shoulder to give them a kiss on the cheek will result in one of the two later being stabbed in the back.

knife

Although a very ordinary implement in daily domestic life, a knife can also be involved in danger — and in superstitions. Possibly the best known is:

Stir with a knife, stir up strife.

The superstitious among us also believe that if any kind of knife is given to someone as a present (before going on a hunting trip for instance, or as a wedding gift) then the friendship is doomed to fail quite soon — it will be 'cut'. But there is a way out. If the recipient of the knife gift is aware of the superstition, he/she will immediately give a coin to the gift-bearer — any coin at all, no matter how tiny. This indicates that the knife was 'bought' and thus no longer retains its evil quality of being able to destroy the friendship. The savvy giver will tape a small coin to the knife itself before handing it over — thus allowing the receiver to return 'payment' on the spot — at least in token. The friendship is then safe.

A superstition which surfaces in America alerts the cook to the danger of chopping food with a knife — when the food is already in the pot.

See also **engagement**; **iron**; **table**.

1

ladder

Walking under a ladder brings bad luck. By the law of averages, one person in a hundred who walks under a ladder might face disaster, while the other ninety-nine will have a normal day. But resistance remains.

In Christian theology, the Almighty is perceived as a factor of three, otherwise known as the Holy Trinity. When a ladder leans against a wall, it forms the shape of a triangle, and to the very sensitive, walking *through* a triangle shows disrespect for the Trinity and will bring bad fortune.

A second theory is more gruesome. In the days of public hangings, the framework from which the noose (or nooses) hung was of necessity very high. The person to be hanged had to climb up the ladder to reach the noose which would end his life. Again, the ladder against the high bar of the gallows formed a triangle — but more importantly, anyone walking under the ladder would be unpleasantly close to a gruesome scene — maybe even close to an already dead body hanging there.

Both explanations are plausible. But for the nervous, there are prescribed antidotes for having inadvertently walked under a ladder:

- Cross your fingers and keep them crossed until you see a dog.
- Spit over your left shoulder.
- Spit on your shoe . . . and don't look at it again until you're sure the spit has dried.

ladybird

A charming little visitor, should one land on you, and it brings good luck. But not if you brush it off — the luck will vanish. Only a gentle puff is permissible.

lamp post

When a couple is walking down the street holding hands and an obstacle (like a lamp post) is ahead, a superstitious couple should not separate and walk around it, one on each side. Even if they rejoin hands on the other side, the brief separation is a signal that the relationship is about to split up. But help is at hand: the negative vibe of the brief separation can be cancelled if, on rejoining hands, they immediately say 'Bread and butter'.

launching a ship with champagne

This popular custom is derived from an ancient superstition that before a newly built craft put to sea, it was necessary to propitiate the gods of the ocean with some sort of sacrifice, so its bows were smeared with human or animal blood. Greeks and Romans followed the tradition but modified the sacrifice, so before the craft was launched red wine was splashed over the craft and it was given a female name. Thus Neptune and Poseidon (who seem to be the same person actually, just in different cultures) would regard it as a symbolic 'wife' and treat it well — reminded by the female figure on the prow.

leaf

Plants which at various times have been declared 'unlucky' to
have inside the house form a rather long list:

> honeysuckle; ivy; hawthorn; bonsai; snowdrops; arum
> lilies; hoya; tradescantia (the purple kind); frangipani;
> lilac; chrysanthemum . . .

Chrysanthemums are believed to summon the ghost of Okiku,
who worked in a samurai's mansion as a serving girl but
resisted his attempts to seduce her — until he threatened to
announce quite falsely that she was a thief, at which Okiku in
despair drowned herself. So it's quite a responsibility having
chrysanthemums inside — since this will cause her ghost the
effort of coming back and haunting your house.

But there's good news: dead leaves of autumn which blow into
your house bring excellent luck with them, but only if they blow
in unaided. Gathering them yourself and bringing them in doesn't
work — in fact it reverses the luck.

The leaf of the bay tree offers an alternative solution to the 'he
loves me, he loves me not' problem. Any young woman facing such
a dilemma can scratch the initials of the man she hopes to attract
onto a bay leaf and wear it inside her shoe for a whole day. If at
day's end the initials are clearer than they were when originally
scratched, her love is secure.

See also **bay**.

Leap Year proposals

The observance of a 'leap year' is thought to have eventuated in
order to balance a calendar/season discrepancy which would
otherwise have arisen. It is this 'rebalancing' which appears to
underpin the custom that women can reverse the usual male
proposal of marriage during a leap year.

An apocryphal story credits 'unmarried Queen Margaret of Scotland with making a legal decree in 1288, that in a leap year a woman could propose marriage.' Pleasing though the story is, the National Archives of Scotland state firmly that 'no such statute exists' and that anyway there was *no* Queen Margaret of Scotland in 1288. So goodbye to that explanation.

Another explanation, even more unlikely, is that the nun later known as St Bridget begged St Patrick to allow women the dignity of being able to propose marriage. After much argument, Patrick decreed that it could happen every fourth year — upon which Bridget immediately proposed to *him*. Patrick declined, but the die was cast and the 'four year' cycle was established.

The truth is — nobody knows how the custom arose. No legal requirement exists for any proposal of marriage on any day.

lemon

An unmarried woman may care to follow an ancient superstition which will foretell her future matrimony or lack of it. The peel from a lemon must be hidden in the woman's armpit for a whole day. That evening she must rub the lemon peel on the four corners of her bed. If a lover is destined to come her way, a vision of him will appear during the night. No vision? No lover.

lettuce

Unlikely though it seems, the humble lettuce has had a long history as an aphrodisiac and was often used in potions to promote passion. Less romantically, lettuce was believed by ancient Romans to prevent drunkenness.

See also **ivy**.

lightning

Long believed to show the anger of the gods, lightning has been the subject of many superstitions. For example, dogs' tails do not, as is often believed, attract lightning. Another common belief is that lightning never strikes the same place twice, but this simply isn't true — it quite often does. The United States National Weather Service reports that New York's Empire State Building is hit by lightning nearly 100 times a year.

Venturing into the territory of faith, rather than superstition, is the belief that the Virgin Mary created lightning in order to give a few seconds' warning before the occasional dangerous wrath of Satan (known as thunder) was visited on earth. Her lightning would give people a few seconds to cross themselves before Satan's evil struck.

See also **bay tree**.

lily

The ancient Greeks worshipped Hera as the Queen of Heaven, the wife of Zeus, the Olympian King of Gods. Zeus had a child out of wedlock but wanted it to have royal inheritance, so he placed it on the breast of his sleeping wife, and magically her breasts produced milk. But Hera suddenly awoke, and finding the unknown baby, pushed it aside. Some drops of her breast milk fell to the ground — and the world's first lilies grew.

Regardless of their accidental origin, lily flowers are blessed with various virtues. They can represent virtue and innocence in a wedding bouquet, and also at a funeral — as a symbol that the innocence of the deceased person has now been restored. Furthermore, in both these circumstances the lily can guard against the forces of evil wanting to upset the proceedings.

Planted in the household garden, the blooms of the lily will deter ghosts. Its bulbs, roasted in hot ash and cut into thin slices, then applied hot onto warts or boils, will hasten their disappearance. But not all is purity and helpfulness. Should you care to mix lily blooms with the sap of a bay tree and place the mix in manure until rotten, evil worms will grow in the mix. Slipping one of these creatures into the pocket of someone you don't like will cause them rampant insomnia.

lily of the valley

It would seem that nothing is free of the ability to bring either good or bad luck — or both. Charming little lilies of the valley owe their origin to either:
⊙ tears wept by the Virgin Mary, or
⊙ blood lost by St Leonard when he was fighting the last dragon in England.

But the tiny blooms are white and have hanging heads — both bad omens. Planting a bed of them in a garden is tempting fate . . . there will be a death within a year.

love

Probably no other topic encourages faith in superstitions more than love. They are most commonly used either to identify in advance who Fate has allocated to you as a partner, or to discover whether the person for whom you feel affection is likely to return the feeling and be your life partner.

But should true love eventuate, there are superstitions with nefarious ways of endangering its course, such as:

⦿ Being photographed together before the wedding.
⦿ Either party buying shoes for the other can result in one person 'walking away' from the engagement.
⦿ Kissing when one partner is sitting down and the other isn't.

And remember, a young woman who takes the last slice of buttered bread from a plate (unless it is specifically offered) is doomed not to experience marriage.

See also **aphrodisiacs**; **apples**; **basil**; **bread**; **eggs**; **engagement**; **four-leafed clover**; **hair**; **Halloween**; **leaf**; **lemon**; **orange**; **pearls**; **playing cards**; **rain**; **St Valentine**.

Macbeth

Shakespeare's play *Macbeth* has long been a worry within
the acting profession. The play is perceived as 'unlucky'. Just
mentioning its title immediately conjures apprehension, so ways
of mentioning it without saying the name have been devised, for
example 'the Scottish play'. It was first performed in the early
1600s, when there was a heightened awareness of witchcraft. Two
monarchs of that time, Elizabeth I and James I, both instigated
the pursuit and destruction of anyone believed to be practising
witchcraft.

Macbeth of course famously features witches, who give out evil
rhymes and predictions. This is thought to be the main reason
behind the centuries-long discomfort theatre people feel about
it. Since its premiere, a suspicion has lurked around the play
that Shakespeare incorporated into it a genuine curse used by
suspected witches of the time. And even though witchcraft has
now largely been consigned to the 'dismissed' basket, there is
still some unease about seeing it.

Furthermore, the plot requires a major fight scene near the
play's end, when actors are getting tired, and accidents within
Macbeth productions seem to occur more often than in other
plays. The apprehension about saying the play's name does not

seem to extend to performing it — it is one of Shakespeare's
most popular plays — and it is only pretending after all. But
mention of the name in 'ordinary conversation' introduces an
unwelcome reminder of the bad times when real witches were
part of the national consciousness and were being tortured
and drowned. Somehow, mentioning *Macbeth* can send a shiver
down some spines.

magpie

The magpie is not the most popular bird in the air and is often
considered unlucky. Magpies have a certain arrogance and air of
menace about them, so it's not difficult to understand that if one
of them is circling your house, then death is approaching. One
way to dispel the portent is to bow to the bird and wish it 'Good
day'. Alternatively, spit over your left shoulder and cry out 'Devil,
I defy thee'.

In some eastern countries the magpie is seen quite differently —
as good luck and not to be harassed. But among English speakers,
its dubious reputation remains. Perhaps the explanation can be
found in an often repeated 'biblical' story (which you won't find
in any Bible) that when all the animals entered Noah's ark, the
magpies refused to go inside and sat on the roof chattering about
how unwelcome they found the whole project.

marigold

The marigold was named in honour of the Virgin Mary, though
there is no evidence (except imaginative) of any connection
between them. But its attractive golden flowers have quite a
bouquet of superstitions regarding their uses:
- The petals are a firm deterrent to witches and their evil.
- If in a dream you see marigold flowers in full bloom, wealth is
  coming your way.
- It is yet another member of the long queue of aphrodisiacs.

These can be considered as superstitions — powers beyond the normal. But historically, there is fairly firm evidence for the positive health benefits of marigolds:

⊚ The discomfort of wasp and bee stings can be banished by the application of marigold petals.
⊚ An infusion of the blooms in distilled water soothes inflammation of the eyes.
⊚ The petals infused help all skin problems, including boils, acne and eczema, and will hasten the healing of burns.
⊚ Marigold 'petal juice' will fight fungal infections: ringworm, thrush and athlete's foot.
⊚ An infusion will ease mouth ulcers and toothache.

However, in 1551 herbalist William Turner expressed his disdain at the marigold being used as a treatment to glamourise hair:

> *Some use it to make their heyre yellow with the floure of this herbe, not beyne content with the natural colour, which God hat gyven them.*

But rather less negatively, Hannah Woolley advised in *The Gentlewoman's Companion* (1673):

> *You may also make Conserve of Marigolds, which taken fasting in the morning is very good against Melancholy; cureth the trembling of the heart, and very good against any Pestilential distemper.*

In short, marigold-petal jam eaten first thing every morning will cure depression!

milk

Back in the days when fewer household conveniences were available, if hot milk was required it was boiled in a container over an open fire. A superstition grew that if the milk boiled over and some fell on the coals, then bad luck would come to the house

— unless someone very quickly sprinkled salt on the area.

Arising from this came a conviction that evil fairies love spilt milk, and should any be spilt anywhere in the house, not just the fireplace, the evil fairies would arrive in a flash to enjoy a paddle. And because they took seven days to evict, the household would have seven days of bad luck — unless you spilled some more.

mirror

For many centuries, the soul was perceived as separable from the body, and never so clearly as when seeing one's reflection in a pool or a mirror. The reflection there was believed to be your soul on a brief walkabout from your body. But having been separated for a short time in this way, the soul normally returned home safely to within its owner — unless a water creature snapped the soul into ripples or, in later centuries, a mirror broke.

A broken mirror is the basis of an ancient superstition of untraceably distant origin but impressive longevity that, whether or not the soul has vanished into splinters, the body is going to experience seven years' bad luck. It was believed to be 'seven' because the philosophers of ancient Rome said that a person's state of health moved in cycles of seven years. In this case, the years triggered a bump in the cycle, inaugurating a new seven-year period of unhealthy misfortune. There is a way out though. If the mirror's pieces can be collected, they must be either buried in sacred ground or flung into a flowing stream or river. If these cures are not available locally, the mirror pieces can be held under a water tap turned on full . . . and the bad luck will be washed away!

mistletoe

The social standing of mistletoe dims a bit when you understand what its name means. The plant grows parasitically on high branches of unrelated trees, having germinated there from a seed dropped in the excreta of a bird which has eaten some berries from a distant plant. Renowned etymologist Eric Partridge explains that the word 'mistletoe' means 'dung on a twig'.

Nevertheless, mistletoe established a serious reputation in several ancient cultures, especially among the ancient Greeks, Babylonians, Celts and, notably, Scandinavians.

Some varieties of this undistinguished looking plant are poisonous, but in others the ancients found healing qualities, including aphrodisiac powers, aid to fertility, ease for menstrual discomfort, help against epilepsy, ulcers and poisons — and even assistance in the quest for eternal life!

In the first century AD the Druids viewed the mistletoe as representing a positive form of life, because it could blossom even during the frozen winter. Ancient Babylonians associated it with a rather sedate form of romance. Mistletoe was hung over the temple of their love goddess, outside of which single women would often stand. Men in search of a marriage mate knew they did this and would also frequently linger. There was no kissing — respectable Babylonians didn't kiss on first dates — but the mistletoe was somehow believed to encourage romance.

So how did 'kissing under the mistletoe' develop? There are several versions, but the favourite is a legend from Scandinavia. The Norse god Baldur — son of Odin, god of truth and light — was so beloved by the other gods that they sought to protect him from all the dangers of the world. His mother Frigg, the goddess of love, went to all the animals and plants of the natural world, as well as to fire and water, iron and all metals, stones and earth, all trees, sicknesses and poisons, and all four-footed beasts, birds and creeping things, to secure an oath from all of them that they would not harm Baldur. Thus the handsome god was deemed invincible.

But the mistletoe was so high in the trees where it lodged that Frigg had neglected to consult with it. So the scheming god Loki made an arrow from the plant and arranged for it to be used to kill the otherwise invincible Baldur. But, in a sunnier postlude of the myth, the gods were able to resurrect Baldur from the dead. The tears of Baldur's mother Frigg became the berries of the mistletoe plant — and Frigg then declared mistletoe to be a symbol of love and would place a kiss on anyone who passed under it.

See also **thirteen**.

moles

A profuse set of superstitions can be summoned up about moles (the type which grows on skin). Most of them are predictions of a person's disposition or future, depending on which part of the body they are located.

Chin: riches will come — 'A mole on the chin, never beholden to any kin.'
Front of the neck: good news, good life.
Back of the neck: bad news, probably a bad end.
Nose: a frequent traveller.
Lip: a great talker . . . or enthusiastic eater.
Right shoulder/arm/foot: luck attends.
Left shoulder/arm/foot: luck steers well away.
Stomach: a glutton.
Shoulder: fortitude.
Thighs: poverty and sadness.
Wrist: an agile mind.
Forehead, right side: riches and honours.
Forehead, centre: sign of a cruel disposition.
Forehead, left side: unlucky, but with a bright intelligence.

Elbow: love of travelling.
Arm, between elbow and wrist: trouble in mid-life, then
  comfort later.
Buttocks: very low ambition.

money

Cash boxes and purses should never be allowed to become empty,
because then the devil will creep in and prevent any further
money being made.

moon

Many superstitions revolve around the moon.

It's unlucky to point at the moon — and if you do it nine times or
more, Heaven will not let you in when you die.

When there's a new moon, you should avoid looking at it through
glass (but spectacles are all right). It's best if you look at it over
your left shoulder, but then you should give it a respectful bow
(the über-respectful bow nine times). And coins in the pocket
should be turned over whenever you see the moon.

In more earthly terms, the rhythm of the moon waxing and
waning can be the signal for many practical activities: planting
at the change of seasons, tree pruning, animal tail-docking, hair
cutting, the removal of foot corns. It also provides an original
way of curing warts: find a moderately shiny metal basin (silver
would be perfect), put water in it, tilt it so the moon shines into
the basin — and vigorously wash your hands.

The position of the moon dictates the timing of certain festivals.
For example, the date of the Christian celebration of Easter each
year is decided by the position of the moon.

Our word 'lunatic' is related to the moon. Derived from the Latin *lunaticus*, meaning 'struck by the moon', the English word 'lunatic' originally meant 'affected with periodic insanity, dependent on the changes of the moon.' Some believe that even the most sensible people can be struck by lunacy if they sleep out under the moon.

moustache

An American folk superstition warns:

Beware of that man,
Be he friend or brother,
Whose hair is one colour
And moustache is another.

nails

If you suspect someone of being a witch, one way of testing it
is to drive an iron nail into one of their footprints. If the person
comes back soon after and withdraws the nail, then the answer is
yes. But if they don't arrive and the nail remains, you were wrong.

An iron nail might help cure the pain of toothache. Place the nail
on the affected tooth, then take it (the nail) and hammer it flat
into nearby ground. The toothache will be transferred to the first
person who walks over it!

names

Besides identifying an individual, everyone's name has an effect
of 'melding into' that person's identity and character. Many
names have a meaning, and parents who are aware of this may
choose a name which they think will aid the child's development
into the qualities the name represents, though this sometimes
proves elusive. Such a choice of a name may have some sort of
effect — for good or bad — when joined to a particular person
who grows in a 'different direction'.

In some cultures a superstition discourages the naming of a
new child after a sibling, previously deceased. There is also a

superstitious danger in naming a new child with the same name as one of its parents, as this could confuse Fate about which one has reached its die-by date.

Naming advice includes watching what the initials might stand for (as someone called Virginia Donald or Bruce Oliver might find). Many people deliberately change their name (either legally or on movie posters) in order to fit the persona they aspire to or have grown into. Thomas Mapother just doesn't sound as crisp as Tom Cruise.

Sometimes parents elect to give a child the same name as a celebrity, although there is no guarantee that the name will influence the child's future in the same direction. The new Samson might become a computer programmer and a new Beyoncé might not be able to sing. Whatever forename is decided on, an ancient superstition advises it must be kept entirely secret until the 'naming ceremony' of the faith elected by the parents. The reason for the discretion is that witches and other evil beings, hearing the child's name mentioned before it is officially named, can thus access the child's identity and (should they feel inclined) cast spells upon it.

It has been usual for women to adopt a new surname when marrying — their husband's, but in many places this is just 'customary'; there is no legal necessity.

See also **baptism; christening**.

narcissus (jonquil)

This flower is named after the mythical Greek man Narcissus, a handsome hunter whose interest in his own good looks led him to gaze into still pools of water to see how handsome he was. Eventually he fell in one and was drowned, whereupon he was transformed into a flower with a lovely perfume.

Some people, conscious of the flower's unfortunate origin, decried the bloom's scent as causing headaches, madness, even death. In time, however, people forgot about the unfortunate Narcissus drowning in his own reflection and the blooms became a spring favourite.

needle

Should you ever feel inclined to say the word 'needle' first thing in the morning, note that it is considered unlucky. Furthermore, if ever a friend asks if they can borrow a needle, you should prick yourself with it before handing it over, in order to protect the longevity of the friendship.

new roof

In building construction, 'topping out' (sometimes referred to as 'topping off') is established as a builder's rite. It is based on an old custom, traditionally held when the last beam (or its equivalent) is placed atop the structure of the roof frame.

The action is derived from a Scandinavian superstition dating back to an era when most buildings were made of wood. After building a (wooden) roof frame, a small tree would be mounted on top as a gesture of respect and appeasement to the spirits of the trees who had been rendered homeless as a result of the tree-felling for the building.

Over time, the original significance of the practice was lost and it was extended to buildings of masonry, iron, bricks, steel and any other material. Their buildings still all need a roof.

As well as the placement of a tree on the roof's completed frame, 'topping off' is usually accompanied by a celebration of some kind: drinks for the builders, maybe a festive meal. However, the custom isn't universal. It was taken up enthusiastically in America, where it is sometimes referred to as 'roof-tree raising' or 'roof-bush raising'. And while the importance of completing the roof remains as significant as ever (a builder asked about the ritual said pragmatically, 'It means we can now work under shelter'), the fact is that many buildings are now much higher than they were in ancient Scandinavia.

For this reason, although a small tree may be taken up to the roof frame of a new skyscraper, it is often there in partnership with a large American flag. This announces to all and sundry, many floors below, that the roof frame has been 'topped off'. Sometimes a 'media event' is held with VIP visitors to announce the near-completion of a major new business enterprise.

New Year

Our current calendar underwent several changes before settling down into its now familiar form. One of these was the beginning of the year, which wasn't always where it is now. Nevertheless, the concept of a 'New Year' captured peoples' urge to celebrate, whatever the date, and ancient rituals and a sense of 'facing the future' have lasted through the centuries.

There are many superstitions based around New Year:
- As midnight approaches, noisy celebrations, bell-ringing, party-singing and plenty of noise at the stroke of midnight are descended from a centuries-old superstition that the noise will act to drive bad spirits away, and thus get the New Year off to an evil-free start.
- Just before midnight on New Year's Eve, open all the doors of the dwelling to let the old year out.
- Kissing at midnight ensures that affections and ties will continue throughout the New Year.
- American New Year's Eve includes a superstitious recommendation to eat as many green vegetables as possible. This is a harbinger that in the New Year to come, plenty of 'greens' will come your way — meaning dollar bills.

Then on New Year's Day, immediately after midnight comes 'first-footing'. This superstition involves the belief that the future of the household depends on the first person to step over the threshold after midnight has struck. Ideally he (the visitor is perceived a 'he') should be dark-haired (blond or ginger brings bad luck) and he must not be cross-eyed or have eyebrows that meet. He should also carry some salt, a piece of coal, some bread and a small amount of money.

The salt and bread symbolise flavour and food for the coming year, the coins represent portents of prosperity, and the coal stands for warmth (and is placed on the fire immediately, while the family makes silent wishes).

If no first-footer shows up, the house owner can do the job himself, but he must carry the same symbolic items in order to bestow good fortune and prosperity on the house for the coming twelve months.

During the day itself, various superstitions impose restrictions:
- Avoid crying. Breaking things or crying and wailing on the first day of the year are likely to continue as a pattern for the rest of the year.
- Do not let anything leave the house on New Year's Day. This includes going out wearing your jewellery, paying off loans, lending things to anyone, even putting the rubbish out. If you plan to deliver presents to family on New Year's Day, place them in the car the day before. That way, you're not taking them out of the house on the day of your visit!
- The superstitious do not wash dishes or do laundry on New Year's Day. This will lead to a death in the family.
- Besides being a day of fun and festivity, doing a little bit of work on New Year's Day will guarantee to the spirits that you are diligent and will prosper.
- Knives, scissors and anything else sharp are not used in Chinese houses at New Year. They 'cut off' the prosperity the coming year should bring.

- The direction of the wind at sunrise on New Year's morning can prophesy fine weather and prosperity if the wind comes from the south, but things will be bad if it comes from the north. An easterly wind brings natural calamities, and a westerly promises good things for most — but the death of an important person as well. If there's no wind at all, the year will be calm and joyous.

If the first butterfly you see in the New Year is white, you will have good luck for the next twelve months. But the most pleasant superstition of all is that babies born on 1 January are said to be the luckiest of all throughout their lives.

There is no known superstition attached to the making of 'New Year resolutions' — vows to improve something in your life — but the custom of doing so is based on similar ancient practices. In Babylon, at the start of a New Year, the citizens promised their gods they would repay debts and return borrowed items. And for Romans, the god Janus who presided over the changing of the year, was the focus of worthy promises at this time of year.

In medieval times, when Christmas was over knights took a vow to reaffirm their commitment to chivalry.

Around the world, New Year has occasioned a variety of beliefs and customs:
- In Denmark, people keep any crockery which has been broken during the year, gather it on New Year's Eve and throw pieces at friends' doorways. The amount of smashed china which piles up at your door is a sign of how many loyal friends wish you luck for the New Year.
- In Italy, wearing red underwear on New Year's Eve helps bring good luck to you all through the coming year. But in Mexico, forthcoming good luck is attracted by underwear of a different colour: yellow.
- In Brazil, wearing white on New Year's Eve will help bring

happiness during the following twelve months. But if you'd like money as well, make sure you eat lentils on New Year's Day.

◉ In Spain, when midnight strikes on New Year's Eve many people eat twelve grapes — one on each time stroke — to ward off evil and bring a year's prosperity.

◉ In parts of Eastern Europe, unmarried women sit in a circle on New Year's Eve with a pile of corn grains in front of each of them. A rooster is then placed in the middle of the circle. If the rooster approaches a woman and starts to eat her pile of corn, then she will be the first to be betrothed in the coming year.

◉ Colombians take an empty suitcase and walk around the streets with it on New Year's Day, in the belief that this will bring adventures and travel in the coming twelve months.

nightmares

According to superstition, nightmares are caused by the devil and his little helpers stealing into your room in order to cause you distressing dreams.

Language scholars explain that the word 'nightmare' has nothing to do with horses. For many centuries there was a belief that a special kind of evil spirit waited for people to sleep, at which time it settled on their prone bodies and sent evil waves into their unconscious minds. In Latin this creature was called an *incubus*, an evil spirit that smothers you, from the Latin *incubare*, to lie on (as in the modern word 'incubate').

Strangely, however, the English language for once didn't borrow the Latin word, but used an Old Norse word *maere*, which also means 'an evil spirit that smothers you'. Gradually the pronunciation turned into *mara*, then a night-*mare*: the night-time *evil spirit*. Don't blame the horses.

Either way, there are methods of avoiding nightmares:

1. Uplift a nail of some kind from a grave, then place it within the frame of the door.

2. If your shoes go under the bed, their toes must be pointing outwards.
3. In bed, wear coral beads, which must be red (bad-dream demons don't like red).
4. Place socks/stockings/tights into the shape of a cross at the end of the bed.
5. Better still, attach small crosses to each corner of the bed.

nine lives *See* **cats**.

nutmeg

One superstition about nutmeg is strangely attractive — and very easy to carry out. Grated nutmeg when sprinkled on an important document will bring success to the document (and by definition, we presume that this includes lottery tickets).

olive oil

Like nutmeg, a superstition involving olive oil is comparatively easy to carry out. A man dissatisfied with his level of virility can find improvement in the kitchen cupboard: drink a slug of olive oil for an unbroken nine mornings — virility will improve!

See also **impotence**.

opals are unlucky

In terms of superstition, the opal has had a bad rap. Because of its beautiful scintillating colours, it was once perceived as being like a rainbow and therefore symbolising good fortune. In fact, one legend about the opal's origin tells that ancient gods were jealous that the rainbow god had command of such beautiful colours so they attacked the rainbow. They didn't succeed in destroying it completely, but the pieces which fell to earth became opals!

Ancient Romans admired the ever-changeable opal, and saw in it a combination of all precious stones: the total of all their colours on display. Opals were seen as representing hope and purity, and were carried as 'attractors' of good fortune. Greek, Arabian and various eastern cultures all also held the opal in high esteem.

onions

Witches don't like onions, so keeping one or two in the house is a good protection — but left whole, not peeled or cut.

However, there is an ancient belief that a peeled onion will 'absorb' germs, thus shortening the span of an illness by taking all the danger into itself and preventing others in the household from catching the affliction. Modern medical experts have advised that because something has been believed for a long time does not mean it is true, and the 'cut onion' information is not true and should be disregarded.

The American National Onion Association (founded in 1913) officially represents the growers, shippers, brokers and commercial representatives of the US onion industry. And although onion growers might have viewed the legend as helping to increase sales and gain respect for their product, the Association has publicly announced: 'There is no scientific evidence that a cut raw onion absorbs germs or rids the air of toxins/poisons.'

But in parallel to such high regard, contrary views grew. Somehow, the opal's inherent multi-coloured quality came to be seen by some to represent inconstancy. And in an era when witches and sorcerers were regarded as real, stories circulated that they used black opals to focus on someone they wanted to harm. There was talk of the colourful opal resembling the Evil

Eye, and it was compared to the eyes of snakes and toads. Claims were even made that it could make wrong-doers invisible. Bishop Marbod of Rennes wrote in 1096:

Tis the guardian of the thievish race; It gifts the bearer with acutest sight;
But clouds all other eyes with thickest night.

Two hundred years later, alchemist Albertus Magnus labelled the opal the 'patron of thieves'. The opal was blamed for earthquakes, tidal waves and the Plague. During the 1700s and 1800s it fell further out of favour and was blamed for sickness and famine. The collapse of several monarchies was blamed on whoever gave a present of opals.

Sir Walter Scott's novel *Anne of Geierstein* (1829) contributed a great deal to the widespread perception that opals bring bad luck — on fairly slender (and fictional) grounds. His character Lady Hermione is depicted as wearing a stunning opal in her hair. At one point some drops of holy water were sprinkled onto her, at which the opal instantly lost all its colour and Lady Hermione faded overnight to a small heap of ashes.

Queen Victoria ignored the nay-sayers. She liked opals and wore them all her life, even at her wedding. Anyone else who likes opals can follow her example: an inanimate stone is unlikely to cause famine, floods or a tidal wave.

orange

Beyond its obvious attraction as a tasty fruit, the orange is central to an old superstition which has become a custom without causing a ripple. Brides often chose to include real or imitation orange blossom in their bridal garb, perhaps not realising that the custom is descended from an ancient superstition that orange blossom will bring happiness — and children — to a married couple's future.

But long before walking down the aisle, if a young man wants to test whether or not the girl he loves returns the feeling, he must take a skewer and make holes all over an orange, then sleep with it under his armpit. The following day, he offers it to the young lady he fancies. If she eats it, the romance is all on!

orchids

Orchids are associated with images of luxury, romance and exotic beauty, but it is rarely observed that the word 'orchid' is from an old Greek word orchis, meaning 'testicle', because of the appearance of the orchid tubers. The association between tubers and testicles may be seen in a colourful superstition. A woman who wants to monitor her man's sexual athleticism can do so with a supply of orchid tubers. To excite him, she should grind a large tuber into the milk he drinks. But to slow him down a bit, replace the large tuber with a small one — and continue as before.

oysters

Apart from the ancient belief that oysters have aphrodisiac qualities, there is another old and fairly breathtaking superstition about the oyster which came to be believed in Yorkshire. Insert some saliva inside both halves of an empty oyster shell, then close the shell carefully and bury it for two days. Dig it up, open carefully, then slowly drop some saliva into each ear — to cure deafness!

parsley

It is now considered an inoffensive herb, but parsley was long held by the ancients to be symbolic of death. In earlier times, there was considered to be a link between parsley and the Devil, and a similarly old belief was that only a wicked person could grow parsley. Historically associated with death and the Devil, planted parsley seed is seen by some as needing to go to the Devil seven times before germinating.

Time has lessened most of parsley's bad reputation, but some people are still reluctant to plant it in a domestic garden lest it cause a relative to die. But Christianity modified the parsley plant into domestic acceptance and cleared away its bad reputation — if the seeds were planted on Good Friday, when the soil is free from Satan's interference.

Having been cleansed of its earlier shady image, parsley was fed to unhealthy sheep and tossed into fish tanks to aid ailing fish. And William Turner's *New Herball* (1551) advises that parsley seed:

> *taken beforehand helpeth men that have weyke braynes to beare drinke better.*

palmistry

Telling a person's future by examining the underside of their hands is a superstition with a rather patchy reputation for accurate results. The shape and characteristics of each finger, allied with the lines criss-crossing the palm, are the evidence the palmist uses in order to 'read' the character of the hand-owner and assay what lies ahead for them.

The practice has been traced back to the Stone Age, and early evidence for it can be found in ancient Sanskrit writings. Palmists gathering around the baby Buddha were reported to be delighted that his hands bore the marks of future greatness. The Bible mentions 'palms' several times as the repository of information:

> *Length of days is in her right hand, and in her left hand riches and honour.* (Proverbs 3:16)

To the comfort of the chiromancers (palm readers), the Kennedy Galton Centre (part of the University of London), after considerable research and examination, has cautiously put forward the result of studies that it is possible to ascertain certain health factors by examining the hands.

A sprig on a meal is believed to help 'bring good will' — and is also an antidote to any poisoning which might accidentally take place at dinner. Moreover, anyone suffering from rheumatism can chew that same sprig to ease rheumatic pain.

Parsley seeds are regarded favourably. Eating some before a riotous evening is believed to be yet another protection against later drunkenness, and parsley seeds sprinkled on the head three times a year are reputed to stave off baldness.

See also **ivy**; **drunkenness**.

pea
If your peas don't come frozen in a bag from the supermarket, but are actually shelled out of their pods within the household, watch out for any pod which contains either just one pea — or nine, for good luck will then come to you. And if the pod which housed nine peas is rubbed on a wart, it will cure it . . . or so the superstition says.

peacock
Although revered in Hindu and other traditions as regal and sacred, the peacock has come under fire in some cultures. The main reason for this is that its brilliantly coloured tail features what look like many eyes — plural depictions of 'the Evil Eye' of superstition and legend. The 'eyes' have at least two interpretations:

- that they are the offspring of the seven deadly sins — and those sins are hovering over peacock territory, waiting to get their eyes back.
- that the tails have a relationship with the legendary giant Argus of ancient Greek legend, who had 100 eyes, and thus formidably never slept with them all shut at once — some were always alert.

pearls

Pearls have a colourful past. Some superstitions gloomily align pearls with tears. But contrarily, another more cheerful superstition advises giving a pearl as a present to a baby, who will then grow into good luck. So will brides who have pearls somewhere about them on their wedding day. Except that in the contrary way which superstitions often have, other gloomy souls quote a different superstition that pearls on a bride will bring tears in the marriage.

But, for anyone who needs a little encouragement in matters of love, sleeping with a pearl under the pillow is believed to be an aphrodisiac.

So the upshot is: you can't get away with any skulduggery while a peacock is watching.

pepper

Here are a few things to bear in mind about pepper:
- Red pepper put deliberately under your carpet will bring you good luck.
- But if any pepper is spilt elsewhere, there will soon be a serious argument between you and your best friend. This can be forestalled, however, by mixing another pinch of pepper with some salt and throwing the mix over your left shoulder.
- In America, Nebraskans have faith in curing earache by dipping some cotton wool in ground pepper and placing it in the ear.

picture

Among the superstitious, there is general nervousness should a picture fall off a wall without any obvious cause. However, there are two conflicting interpretations of the outcome:

1. There will be bad luck in the household, probably a death.
2. There will be no death and nothing ominous will occur unless the picture's *glass breaks*.

The nervousness goes back to an ancient belief that the painted portrait of a person 'captured' something of that person's spirit, so damage to the portrait was a bad omen for the well-being of its subject. Historic portraits rarely had glass, so that branch of the belief must be a modern adaptation.

See also **mirror**.

pin

The humble pin is the subject of the old rhyme:

> *See a pin and pick it up,*
> *All the day you'll have good luck.*
> *See a pin and let it lie,*
> *Luck will surely pass you by.*

But that's not the full story. The deep-dyed fan of superstition will tell you that you should only pick up the pin if it's facing *away* from you. If it's facing *towards* you, leave it where it is.

Also, just like St Anthony, a pin can help you find something you've lost. You stick it into any cushion, and say: 'I pin you, my devil.' (And as with St Anthony, there may well be some explanation as to why this doesn't always work.)

See also **brides; needle**.

playing cards

There are so many superstitions about playing cards that to cite them all would require a whole book, but here are a few:

- To be lucky at cards means you'll be unlucky in love.
- Unlucky cards are: knave and four of clubs; knave and ace of spades; nine of diamonds.
- Ace of hearts signifies wealth.
- Beginners at card games often have luck (short-lived).
- A cross-eyed person at the gaming table will not add any luck.
- Losing your temper during a game is unlucky.
- So is singing!
- If a used matchstick is thrown on the ashtray, place another one crossways over it — and win.
- When good luck seems to have deserted a player, he can reverse this by standing, taking up his chair and walking with it in a circle three times.

See also **cards**.

pointing the finger

Frequently regarded as rude, the pointing of a finger at someone is based on an ancient superstition rather more dangerous than rude. The ancients believed that the pointed finger attracted evil spirits passing by, whose random gathering together formed an extremely dangerous force — an assembly of evil which your pointing finger was transmitting to someone else. So powerful can this assembled force be that men of the sea avoided pointing even at a boat (always vulnerable to unpredictable sea accidents).

Curiously, any danger is avoided if pointing is done with the whole hand.

poplar trees

Poplar leaves shiver in the slightest breeze, but more importantly, they are an ingredient in the potion brewed by witches to enable them to fly.

rabbits

Quite innocently, the rabbit has been allocated a role in many
superstitions which attempt to influence the role of luck — good
or bad.

When out and about in the countryside, seeing a black rabbit
cross your path is a sure sign of good fortune coming your
way. But the reverse applies — bad fortune — if a black rabbit
crosses *behind* you. (It isn't fruitful to query the validity of a
superstition, but this one raises the fairly obvious question: how
would you know if a black rabbit crossed behind you?) However,
whether you ever see real rabbits, black or otherwise, your
fortune can still be influenced by them.

A superstition of dubious origin advises that on the first day of
every month, by saying the words 'white rabbit' out loud as the
first words uttered upon waking, good luck will follow for the
following thirty days. But the devil is in the detail, and several
variations have evolved. Should it be plural: 'white rabbits'?
And will it still work if you say just 'rabbits'? What about the
variation that you must say the words three times? And some
people say that in order to be effective, 'black rabbits' must be
the last words you utter before going to sleep — a necessary
prelude to saying 'white rabbits' in the morning.

There is one other slightly awkward necessity regarding the night before. If your house has stairs, they must be mounted walking backwards, before going to bed and saying 'black rabbits'. America has modified the first words spoken in the morning to the rather cutesy 'bunny, bunny, bunny'. The jury still appears to be out on which of these requirements is 'correct' — and how effective any of them is.

In the long run, it is easier to court good fortune by complying with the oldest rabbit superstition of all — to carry a rabbit's foot with you at all times. The rabbit's foot represents life moving successfully forward, leaping into the future. But even with this, there are rules to follow. Ideally it should be the left hind foot of a rabbit which has been shot by a cross-eyed man under a full moon! Good luck with that.

See also **cats**.

rain

There are many superstitions about rain. Here are a few of them:

Rain is about to occur if:
> A buttered piece of bread falls face down on the floor.
> For no reason, soot falls down a chimney.
> A cat rubs behind its ears.
> Corns on the feet start to ache.
> Spiders are looking for somewhere to hide.
> Fern plants are cut or burned.
> Flour is thrown into a spring, then stirred with a plant rod.
> You step on a beetle.
> A religious relic is dipped in holy water.

And to stop rain, there's the ancient poem:

> *Rain, rain go away, come again another day.*

Or:

Rain, rain go to Spain, never come back here again.

If that doesn't work, an old superstition recommends persuading a co-operative first-born child to undress and stand on his or her head in the middle of the rain. This will cause the rain to stop.

Don't complain about rain at a funeral — it heralds the fact that the deceased's soul has departed to a better life.

But without doubt the two most intriguing superstitions about rain are:
⊚ Money which has been washed in fresh rainwater will never be stolen.
⊚ Couples making love while it is raining will conceive a girl child.

rainbow
Rainbows are a phenomenon of nature and occur all over the world, so it is not surprising that they have different legends and their significance varies among cultures. The Burmese, Zulus, Australian Aborigines, Indians, Finns, Austrians, Maoris, Armenians, Buddhists, Chinese, Bulgarians and Arabs — to name but a few — all have their own stories.

Among these is the Jewish interpretation of the rainbow, in the account of Noah who saved the animals from a great flood. When it was over, the book of Genesis recounts God's promise:

I do set my bow in the cloud, and it shall be for a token of a covenant between me and the earth. The waters shall no more become a flood to destroy all flesh. (Genesis 9:13)

From there developed two notable superstitions:
⊚ It is dangerous to point a finger at the rainbow, since the pointer will experience misfortune and the rains will return.
⊚ There will be a pot of gold waiting at the point where the

rainbow ends and touches the ground. (Nobody has ever found the place.)

See also **opals**; **gold**.

rats

Rats seldom get a good press. For centuries there was a belief that rats were able to predict the sinking of a ship (though this is believed to happen while the ship is moored near land — before leaving for a rat-predicted doomed voyage). Similarly they might desert a household *en masse*, which is not good news for those who believe that rats can foretell when the building is about to collapse — or that someone in it is about to die.

On the other hand, if rats are showing no intention of leaving a property, but the householders wish they would, two superstitions are on offer which might be effective:

◉ **Write a note**. If you can think up a curse which rats wouldn't like — maybe 'May mange affect you and your teeth drop out' — then write it down and leave the paper where there is known to be rat traffic.

◉ **Music**. Yes, the storied power of that piper in Hamelin (first written account 1384) is believed to have a grain of veracity. If you can find the right person to whistle or sing in a way which attracts rats, ask them to do so outside your house and you will be rid of them from your property.

On the plus side, it is believed by some that rats can contribute to curing a bad cold — if you don't mind eating a stew made of rats' tails.

rice *See* **confetti**.

rheumatism

According to superstition, the pain of rheumatism can be alleviated by one of the following cures:

- Carry a rabbit's foot with you (necessarily separated from the rest of the rabbit).
- Put a new potato in your pocket and keep it with you until it turns black and goes rock-hard.
- Bring in some bees and annoy them somewhere near the affected joint so they will sting the area and take the pain away with them.
- If you are truly desperate, undress until naked and have yourself buried upright in a churchyard (only up to the neck of course) for at least two hours. (You will need to ensure that the person who buries you knows to come back later.)

rings

The basis for the customary wearing of rings to denote marriage is the ancient recognition that the circle has no beginning and no end, in other words eternity, unity and perfection. Hence they represent the wish that a marriage will be long and happy.

rose

Superstitions are not sacred to one culture. Sometimes a superstition can leap barriers and take up residence in different areas. Some superstitions about roses illustrate this:

- If you wish, you can believe that roses had no thorns until the expulsion of Adam and Eve from Paradise, when prickles sprang out of their stems.
- Muslim legend believes that roses grew out of beads of sweat

from the Prophet Muhammad.
- Greek legend has Aphrodite, the goddess of love, being born out of the foam of the sea. As she emerged on land, the white foam fell to ground and became white roses.
- Later when Aphrodite ran to tend the injured Adonis, the mixture of his blood and tears formed the beautiful red rose.
- Ancient Rome disagreed. Their story was that the mischievous Cupid knocked over some red wine in a bowl. Where the wine fell to ground, red roses grew.
- In Iran (Persia) a nightingale was so entranced with the beauty of a white rose that she flew too close and a thorn pricked her breast. The drops of blood became red roses.
- Later, Christian symbolism was added to the list. According to a Christian legend, all roses were red until the Virgin Mary took off her cloak on a warm day and rested it on a rose bush, at which all the roses in bloom turned white in recognition of her purity.
- But some red roses must have remained. They came to symbolise the blood of Jesus' crucifixion.

Then there's the connection between roses and romance. Dreaming of roses (preferably red ones) foretells success in romantic endeavour. Dreaming of white roses is not so good — romance will be elusive.

But white roses were ascribed by an unknown authority as the flower of Harpocrates, the god of silence — an association occasionally heard in the phrase *sub rosa* ('under the rose'). In ancient Roman banquet rooms the ceilings often featured painted roses, to remind attendees at power meetings that whatever was said should remain *sub rosa* — silent and confidential. In later centuries, carved or painted roses appeared on the ceilings of council chambers and Christian confessional booths, indicating the privacy of conversations therein.

rosemary

Rosemary has been used for flavouring since at least 500 BC, and has also been gathering legends and superstitions through all the centuries since — both culinary and otherwise. The leaves have an aromatic, slightly bitter taste, used as flavouring in foods such as lamb, duck and chicken. But the plant was also believed to keep the brain alert and lubricate the memory banks. Students in ancient Greece wove sprigs into their hair to help their brains function during exams.

Even when not used in cooking, the crushed leaves give out a slightly pungent but not unpleasant fragrance. Known as 'poor man's incense', it was often spread on the floor so when trodden on the room would have a fragrant smell.

Carrying a sprig of rosemary is also protection against witches, bad fairies, evil spirits, thunder, lightning and assault.

An imaginative addition to the official Bible reports that Mary washed baby Jesus' garments and spread them on a rosemary bush. As a result, the normally white rosemary flowers turned blue — as all rosemary flowers have been ever since.

After the death of Jesus, a legend developed that the rosemary bush would never grow any taller than Jesus — and if it got to that height, it would start bushing out sideways.

The superstitious put sprigs of rosemary into the hands of the deceased before a burial, because besides all its other uses, traditionally rosemary was the guardian of remembrance. As Ophelia reminds us: 'rosemary — that's for remembrance.' Shakespeare got it right.

sage

The common herb sage, freshly harvested, is the subject of one of the more bizarre superstitions. When a family member is away from home, either missing or on legitimate business, a sprig of sage hung in the kitchen will remain fresh as long as that person is safe, but will wither if any mishap befalls them or trouble arises.

Wherever this superstition arose, it would seem that 'safe' journeys must have been fairly brief, because a cut sprig of sage starts to wither after a day and a half.

Santa Claus

How an obscure Turkish bishop came to be the central figure in a major Christmas custom is not due to superstition but is rather a triumph of imagination and marketing. More than a thousand years after he died, the little-known St Nicholas began a metamorphosis into a jolly chimney climber.

Myths and legends and customs over a period of fifteen centuries told of Nicholas's kindness to children and the comfort he showed towards poor families, leading to his being revered across Europe and becoming the patron saint of children and

salt

Useful in cooking and preserving, salt has been valued for several millennia and is associated with many legends. Its 'godly' qualities were known to the Aztecs, and its less welcome qualities were known to Lot's wife at the city of Sodom. It has also been a favourite ingredient for exorcism ceremonies.

According to superstition, accidentally spilling some salt means that tears will be shed for every grain on the ground. But this can be cancelled out by tossing a pinch of it over the left shoulder, where it will hit the devil (that's where he lives).

Another useful trick: when a visitor has proved unpleasant, there's a way of ensuring that they don't return. Discreetly throw some salt after them as they turn their back and walk away from the front door.

The notion of taking a piece of information 'with a pinch/ grain of salt' is less a superstition than a rather garbled descendant of an ancient Roman belief that taking some salt would cancel out a dose of poison. But alas, the word *salis* in Latin also means 'wit', so taking 'a grain of *salis*' could have meant using your superior intellect to scorn something you've been told which you consider very unlikely. The word 'salary' derives from the ancient Roman practice of paying the military *salarium*, an allowance for rations of salt.

Leonardo da Vinci's famous painting of the Last Supper shows Judas spilling some salt, but this is not the origin of the belief that spilt salt is the forerunner of bad happenings. This belief existed long before Leonardo, who apparently used the well-known reputation of spilt salt to add drama to the position of Judas at Jesus' table.

sailors. Dutch people in particular honoured him and held a St Nicholas parade each year. When many people emigrated from the Netherlands to America, they presented their annual St Nicholas parade just as they had done at home.

The transition from the austere Turkish bishop to the money-spinning Santa began with American author Washington Irving's *History of New York* (1809). Irving presented a fanciful and inventive line about St Nicholas, describing him as:

riding over the tops of the trees, in that self-same wagon wherein he brings his yearly presents to children.

Two years later a more influential — and decisive — factor appeared. On 23 December 1823, *The Troy Sentinel*, a small New York newspaper, published a poem by Clement Moore entitled 'A Visit from Saint Nicholas' with the opening line:

'Twas the night before Christmas, when all through the house . . .

The poem established images which Moore had simply invented: chubby figure, fur-trimmed jacket, beard, sleigh, chimney visit — and eight reindeer. In 1863 the first pictorial image of the benevolent old man and his sleigh, exactly as Clement Moore had described him, appeared as a black-and-white drawing in a magazine. The complete image was beginning to unfold. All Moore's invented attributes are with us still.

During an annual St Nicholas parade in New York by Dutch citizens, legend has it that an American newspaper reporter asked a bystander who the stately figure in bishop's robes represented. The answer from the Dutch bystander was the Dutch version of the bishop's name — *Sinterklaas* — which the American journalist mistakenly wrote down as Santa Claus.

This became the turning-point in the transformation of the

austere bishop St Nicholas, who was soon forgotten. From then on the totally reconfigured version of Clement Moore's night-time visitor with a sack of toys and eight reindeer became a major international industry. He had never heard of the North Pole.

St Christopher
He is the patron saint of travellers, but why?

The provenance is very vague. Some say he lived in the third century AD, others say the fourth. Even his name is in doubt: Christopher may also have been called Decius, Reprobus, Dacian or Menas. Nothing is clear.

He is considered to be the patron saint of travellers because of one oft-repeated legend (or myth?) that he once carried baby Jesus over a turbulent river. Alas, the fact that he lived in either the third of the fourth century makes it very unlikely he had any sort of a meeting with Jesus — who had died two hundred years earlier.

But faith is a wonderful thing, and as the passing centuries introduced travel by steam, by motor and by air, so the observance of the 'baby-carrying' legend spread. Christopher was seen as a protector against mishap during all kinds of travel — not just in crossing rivers. Medallions showing him are still frequently seen in vehicles.

St Valentine
Modern commercialism has built a custom which, without the support of any attendant superstitions, has overwhelmed the frail background and minuscule knowledge of the Saints Valentine. And popular belief in their fostering of romance could be based on a mistaken date!

There are eleven Saints Valentine on the Catholic roll of saints. All were Catholic priests, sworn to celibacy and therefore presumably with no first-hand knowledge of romantic love. But besides their unlikely association with romantic love, confusion between the dates of two saints' days somehow instigated a vast, commercial-driven orgy of spending.

The Roman Valentine died in AD 269 and was declared a saint in AD 496 by Pope Gelasius, with a 'saint day' of 14 February. Nobody sent any cards . . . yet.

Another man, Saint Valentine of Genoa, died in AD 307, and his 'saint day' was declared to be 2 May.

For the next 1075 years, nobody seemed to take much notice of any of the eleven Saints Valentine — until Geoffrey Chaucer came along. His amusing *Parlement of Foules* contained one line which eventually formed the basis of a phenomenon which has caused card manufacturers, chocolate makers, restaurants, florists and even the travel industry to rejoice greatly. Chaucer wrote:

For this was on seynt Volantynys day
Whan euery bryd comyth there to chese his make.

For this was on Saint Valentine's day
When every bird comes there to choose his mate.

Such was Chaucer's popularity that the line caught on and the concept of relating St Valentine with 'choosing one's mate' started to grow slowly — and gradually move away from birds.

Over the following 200 years, St Valentine received scant mention. But by 1593 Thomas Nashe was making a closer association between the saint and young lovers:

It was the merie moneth of Februarie
When yong-men in their iollie roguerie
Rose earelie in the morne fore breake of daie
To seeke them valentines so trimme and gaie.

With whom they maie consorte in summer sheene

Note that Chaucer never mentioned a month, or which Valentine — but Thomas Nashe points to February, which means he was referring to the Roman Valentine.

The perception of birds mating was slowly morphing into people mating. Shakespeare took a bet both ways and chose a midstream position. In *A Midsummer Night's Dream* he adheres to the aerial association:

Good morrow, friends — Saint Valentine is past!
Begin these wood-birds but to couple now?

But several years later in *Hamlet* (1603), he changed tack when Ophelia has a romantic thought and sings it to a ballad tune already familiar to Tudor audiences, suggesting that by then Valentine's Day no longer applied just to birds:

Tomorrow is Saint Valentine's day,
All in the morning betime,
And I a maid at your window,
To be your Valentine.

But do birds mate on Valentine's feast day, 14 February, in the middle of the northern winter? No, they do not.

Chaucer never clarified on which day of the eleven Saints Valentine the mating took place. But like many authors of the time, he liked to include the occasional royal reference. And when he wrote the line in *Parlement of Foules*, it is believed he was subtly referring to the anniversary of a royal event of some importance. A year earlier, England's 14-year-old King Richard II was engaged to 14-year-old Anne of Bohemia on 2 May — which is the saint's day of St Valentine of Genoa. Scholars point out that Chaucer could have been connecting the royal occasion with the Valentine whose 'day' is 2 May, when birds in Britain *do* mate.

So it could well be that the chocolate and floral industries have been using all their persuasive powers to make us spend as much as possible to celebrate the wrong saint on the wrong day.

At some point after 1603 the fragile fantasy was fuelled by mass media and reshaped by rampant commercialism. The ancient unknown (and totally bachelor) Saints Valentine were morphed into becoming the focus of an aggressively frenzied framework which we can feel fairly confident the real Valentines had little wish to represent — namely spend, spend, spend! And even if the saint in question is actually the wrong one, this does not cause the populace grief, since any actual connection with a deceased saint has long been abandoned and the retail festival is generally referred to as just Valentine's Day.

No matter how confused the date of the festival has been for over a thousand years, it has gathered some superstitions around it, and the strangest relate to birds. On St Valentine's Day an unmarried girl must pay attention to them. If she sees a robin, she will marry a sailor. If she sees a dove, she will marry a man with a golden heart. Seeing a goldfinch brings promise of a husband who is rich, whereas seeing a humble sparrow means she will marry a husband who, although poor, will bring her constant happiness. But to see an owl means, alas, she will not marry at all.

sciatica

There is a belief, not founded on medical evidence and requiring a generous modicum of faith, that the pain of sciatica can be alleviated by carrying around a knucklebone from a sheep.

seven

Over time, the number seven has had various significances: human life was seen to live through seven ages; rainbows have seven colours; early astrology believed seven planets made up the universe; a seventh child had special powers; a week has seven

scissors

There's a superstition that scissors should always be bought and should never be given as a present, because that will cause a 'cut' between the giver and the recipient. And be aware that if a pair of scissors is dropped, the fates will gather around the person who dropped them if they pick up the scissors themselves — they should ask someone else to pick them up. Worse, if when the scissors fall both points stick into the floor and the scissors remain upright, then a death is imminent. However, a more gentle fate awaits if only one point sticks into the floor — that presages a wedding.

In Egypt it is considered very bad luck to open and close scissors without cutting anything, and even worse, to open them and leave then open.

days; deadly sins have been narrowed to seven; and Oscar Wilde assigned seven veils to Salome (though the Bible doesn't mention them at all).

See also **horseshoe**; **mirror**.

sewing

If even the simplest on-the-go mending takes place while the mender or the mendee is still wearing the garment, superstition rules that bad luck will result. Nor is it wise to start sewing a garment on a Friday, unless you can be sure of finishing it before the day is out.

shaking hands

What we know as 'shaking hands' has been done for at least 2500 years, and possibly earlier. It may have arisen from a gesture indicating 'I come in peace', because it was being made clear that no weapon was being held — at least in the right hand. But some forms of handshake customarily involve the 'other' hand clasping the wrist of the hand being shaken.

The 'coming in peace' explanation doesn't seem to apply to handshakes upon parting, handshakes of congratulation, completing a business transaction or as a sign of good sportsmanship. So whatever its origin, the handshake on occasion can convey equality, admiration, agreement or affirmation of affection.

ships as 'she'

Seagoing vessel are frequently referred to as 'she'. The custom dates back to an ancient superstition held by some cultures (but not all) that vessels at sea needed the protection of a goddess, one of whom often came to be featured as a carving on the prow.

Historically, Viking ships had menacing figureheads to ward off evil spirits. Egyptians often featured birds, and Phoenicians favoured horse figures (suggesting speed). Other sea-going figureheads in past centuries included serpents, dolphins, dragons, a bull, an armoured soldier and the head of a boar. Sometimes it was a graceful swan.

But the imagery of women also played a significant part in ship lore. Whatever its figurehead, many ships were dedicated to various goddesses for protection at sea. Also, the historic absence of women on most ships of industry or war encouraged a fragile conceit that the craft itself was female — the only woman allowed on the high seas.

In 2002, the famous insurance firm Lloyd's of London declared that it would no longer refer to ships as 'she'. Its reasoning was that this would bring it into line with 'most other reputable international business titles', which refer to ships in neutral terms. Lloyds described ships as 'maritime real estate' in which 'she' might suit a magnificent cruise liner but could be rather offensive when referring to a rusting old hulk.

A spokesman for the Royal Navy declared that Lloyds could do what it liked, but the Royal Navy would continue to refer to ships as female, since it is 'historical and traditional'. The British Marine Industries Federation agreed and said it had no plans to change.

shirt

Because the shirt or its equivalent is worn next to the skin, some people believe the garment can absorb some natural vibes from its wearer, so a number of superstitions have accumulated:
- If a small child is showing signs of being peaky, then throwing his or her shirt into water will signal one of the following: (a) if it floats, good health will return, or (b) if it sinks, the wearer's health is in grave danger.
- A shirt's usual wearer must have his wits about him when putting a shirt on. If the shirt is buttoned up wrongly or is pulled on inside out, then be prepared for bad luck. But a shirt put on back-to-front will portend good things to the wearer, but only if it happens accidentally.
- Since the shirt carries its wearer's aura and possible strength, it is wise for a child to wear his father's shirts, but not that of other people whose sins or weaknesses will be carried within the shirt and conveyed onto the wearer. (This optimistically assumes that the father has no sins or weaknesses waiting to be transferred to the child.)

shoes

Through the centuries shoes have carried a great deal of symbolic superstition. Bad luck will come if shoes are ever put on a table (this, for some obscure reason, is connected with convicts usually being hanged with their shoes on).

Some Americans are sure that walking around the house, even from one room to another, while wearing only one shoe should be avoided at all costs, as it will result in the death of either your mother or father.

For the truly dedicated follower of superstition, always putting the left shoe on first will prevent toothache ever happening, and placing shoes under the bed with their soles facing up will fend off night-time cramp. They have been seen as the home of the soul — and as aids to fertility!

When people were beginning a journey it was customary to throw an old shoe at them. It was believed to convey to the travellers all the good luck and experience of the shoe's former owner. (Conveniently, old shoes carried more use and wisdom than new — and of course new shoes are expensive, so there was an economic reason for using old shoes as well.)

As far back as the Bible, shoes have carried a connotation of domination and ruling:

Over Edom itself I cast my shoe. (Psalm 60:8)

At weddings, old shoes signify the bride's father and family transferring ownership or control over her to her new married state — and also good luck and future fertility.

Queen Victoria's diary in 1855 tells that when she and Prince Albert first went to live at Balmoral Castle, an old shoe was thrown after them for luck as they entered the house. When that happened, she and Albert had been married for nearly 15 years, but the throwing of shoes still carried powerful signals of good luck and wisdom. It also signalled their dominion over the new Balmoral Castle.

Influenced by such ancient superstitions, the cultural significance of feet and shoes remains strong. Shoes are tied to a bridal getaway car; members of royalty may not be depicted underfoot on a mat; some religions and cultures prefer shoes to be left outside the door; a metaphor refers to being 'under the boot' of tyranny.

There's also a superstition about slippers. When taken off and put aside, they must always be laid separately, not one atop the other or criss-crossed.

shoelaces

Believe it or not, a quaint old superstition extends as far as the colour of shoelaces. Putting brown laces into black shoes may be considered sartorial doom, but such a practice carries a more sinister message. The colour combination of brown, symbolising the grave's brown earth, when mixed with black, creates the gloom associated with death. So apart from missing out on the best-dressed list, the careless wearer has tempted Fate.

snails

Apartment dwellers who have little contact with these slimy sliders are missing out on a couple of beneficial superstitions about them. The believers say that a period of very good luck will come to those who manage to pick up a snail by its two horns and throw it over their left shoulder.

And yet another way for the unmarried to discover who their future love will be is to put a snail in a flat dish and leave it overnight on 31 October (Halloween). The following morning its slimy perambulations around the dish will form the initials of their future partner!

See also **cough**; **deafness**.

sleep

Apart from the occasional sleeping pill, there is very little one can do to organise how one sleeps, and even less to control how one dreams. Nevertheless, superstitions have been passed down which contrive to bring order and even enhanced value to the ordinary (and logical) rhythm of tired → sleep → dream → wake up.

One much-believed superstition regarding sleep is that the bed should be positioned on a north-south line. Unfortunately, the worth of the belief comes seriously adrift between the two other rival superstitions that (a) one should sleep with the head north and the feet south, or (b) with the feet north and the head south.

A minority of believers discard the north-south bed theory altogether, and in its place stand by beliefs that either (a) sleeping with one's head pointing east will encourage the acquisition of wealth, or (b) that sleeping with head pointing west will bring a life rich with travel.

Should none of the above result in the calm deep sleep they are believed to induce, and in the absence of access to sleeping pills, two ancient superstitions can be invoked which encourage sleep regardless of which way the feet are pointing:
1. Check through the house to see nobody has hung up the wing from a dead blackbird. These creatures have a strong counter-effect on restful sleep, so if one is found, get rid of it.
2. Before bed-time, smoke a pipe filled with a mixture of honey and dried powdered toad.

sneeze

Officially known as 'sternutation,' a sneeze triggers a post-sneeze blessing in at least seventy different languages around the world as an offering of goodwill towards the sneezer. The reasons for this, and the superstitions which apply to sneezing, are numerous. Saying 'Bless you' to someone is a version of the ancient way of politely requesting the Almighty to place his care upon you, dating from ancient Jewish times (see Numbers 6: 24: 'The Lord bless thee and keep thee'). It is frequently invoked when someone sneezes — one of the many superstitions accompanying the involuntary act of sneezing.

In earlier times, beliefs about sneezing were serious:
1. The impact of a sneeze can throw a person's soul out of their body — and a blessing is required to restore it to its rightful place.
2. During a sneeze, the devil and/or evil spirits have an opportunity — no matter how brief — to enter the body, and a post-sneeze blessing will negate their plans.
3. Or the body is already inhabited by an evil spirit which has sneaked in, and a sneeze will hurl it back out.
4. Some believe the heart stops beating during a sneeze (it doesn't), and an immediate blessing will help bring it back into business.
5. Taking a more general view, the English 'Bless you' or the German *Gesundheit* seem to acknowledge that the sneeze is a momentary aberration, and your own good health will take over now the sneeze is over and done with.

In later times, other superstitions were added:
1. If a sneeze manifests itself early in the morning, then later in the day something pleasant in the way of a gift or a message will occur.
2. But if a sneeze occurs before putting one's shoes on, then the day ahead will bring something unpleasant.
3. This could be counter-balanced by the number of sneezes. Two sneezes in quick succession are a message that your luck is in,

but one by itself — or three — and your luck will change for the worse.

4. Those of a cautious nature should carefully follow superstitions which offer advice on the direction in which a sneeze should be aimed. A sneeze straight ahead will bring good news, while sneezing to the right will encourage good luck. But if you sneeze to your left, prepare for bad news, particularly if your left-sneeze is anywhere near a grave.

The citizens of ancient Rome would say the Latin equivalent of 'Preserve you' or 'Save you' as quickly as possible, in order to assist the person's soul back to where it belonged. This would prevent evil spirits from finding their way into the body during the soul's (hopefully brief) absence.

Pope Gregory I is credited with offering a 'God bless' when sneezing was identified as a symptom of bubonic plague (though it could have been Pope Gregory VII — each has been credited). As a descendant of this, saying 'Save you', 'Bless you' or their equivalents had been in use for many years before the Great Plague in London (1665-66). Then, the sneeze took on a more significant and verifiable aspect, because at that time a sneezing fit was a sure symptom that the plague had struck and the person sneezing did not have long to live. Rather than a brief departure of their soul, a sneeze became a sign of a departure of life itself.

At some time during or after the arrival of the plague in Britain, there arose the nursery rhyme:

Ringa-ringa-roses,
A pocket full of posies;
A-tishoo, a-tishoo, we all fall down.

These lines are believed to refer to the red spots which occurred on a plague victim's skin, the herbs which people carried in their pockets as a hopeful deterrent to the disease, and the so-called 'cold' which caused them to sneeze, then shortly 'fall down' — dead.

There is an ancient rhyme which neatly summarises what will happen on the day you sneeze:

Sneeze on Monday, sneeze for danger,
Sneeze on Tuesday, kiss a stranger,
Sneeze on Wednesday, sneeze for a letter,
Sneeze on Thursday, something better,
Sneeze on Friday, sneeze for sorrow,
Sneeze on Saturday, see your sweetheart tomorrow,
Sneeze on Sunday, your safety seek –
The Devil will have you the whole of the week.

One survivor of the complex history of sneeze-significance is related to the seriousness of possible plague symptoms. This is the expression that something is 'not to be sneezed at', meaning that what's being referred to is a matter for serious attention.

soap

This simple accessory to personal grooming has an attached superstition to make you think twice before Mother's Day, or persuade you to do some last-minute shopping before a friend's birthday. It is believed that giving soap as a present will result in the friendship between the giver and the receiver being washed away.

something old, something new

Each part of this old wedding superstition has a meaning:

Something old: provides the bride with a feeling of safety and
    security.
Something new: good luck, aligned with the feeling of pleasure in
    obtaining a new object. It also acknowledges the 'newness' of

life which the marriage will bring.

Something borrowed: it should be something worn by a trusted
female friend who has worn it at a time of her own happiness.

Something blue: represents the sky, which on a good day is blue
and provides a clear path to Heaven. Thus something blue
represents purity and the divine.

spade

Unlikely though it may be to happen today, the impulse to 'carry
a spade into the house over one's shoulder' must be firmly
suppressed. Why? Because a superstition tells us that spades
are used to dig graves and therefore represent death. So casually
carrying one into a house can indicate — you guessed it — that
someone in the house will soon die. The only counteraction for
the unlucky someone is to throw a handful of soil towards the
spade-thrower.

This presupposes that those believing in this old superstition
will keep a supply of soil inside the house for just such an
emergency.

sparrow

Seemingly innocent and obviously harmless, the little sparrow
has an unfortunate reputation.

An old Russian legend added some imaginative creativity to the
New Testament by claiming that when Jesus was in the Garden
of Gethsemane the sparrows assembled and chirruped to alert
the soldiers where he was. And then, during the crucifixion, when
Jesus was believed to have already died, the sparrows chirped
'He's alive, he's alive', alerting the guards to torture him further.

To support and further the impact of these sad myths, a creative
explanation for the sparrow's distinctive hopping motion was
devised. Inventors of the legend decreed that it was a restriction

placed upon sparrows by God, who, as punishment for their betrayals of Jesus, tied their legs together so they could not walk or run.

Over successive centuries, these imaginative 'legends' fuelled a superstition associating the jaunty little bird with death — and the superstitious declared that if one should fly inside a house then major doom was nigh.

Little wonder then that in Mary Cooper's rhyme (1744) we are told it was the sparrow who killed cock robin.

spitting
It may be of doubtful etiquette, but spitting and spit in general have long had a reputation for possessing rather unexpected spiritual qualities. In ancient times the ejection of a bit of spit symbolised the release of part of a person's spiritual soul — in

spiders

For some people spiders have a built-in ability to cause fear and loathing, just by being there. But to the superstitious they manifest the ability to bring you luck! This appears to date from myth-makers again enlarging on the Bible. Missing from the biblical account of Jesus' birth is a tale of mysterious origin: that joy at the birth of the Saviour caused all the spiders to spin webs of silver and gold. Later, the book of Matthew reports the Holy Family's flight to Egypt, but rather sparsely:

When he (Joseph) arose he took the young child and his mother by night and departed for Egypt, and was there until the death of Herod. (Matthew 2: 14-15)

Enter another non-biblical 'legend' enlarging on that incident and the family's escape:

While Joseph, Mary and Jesus hid by night in a mountain cave, a spider industriously worked all night to spin a beautiful web over the cave mouth. When next day Herod's soldiers in their search came to the cave and saw the web, they said, 'There cannot be anyone inside here — they would have broken the web going in.' And so the soldiers passed on. The spider had saved the life of Jesus, Joseph and Mary.

Apparently this charming but non-authorised addition to the Bible's account widened generously to bestow spider-luck on ordinary folk. Hence the proliferation of spider-luck superstitions:

If that you would live and thrive –
Let the spider run alive!

and the remedy:

*Kill a spider, bad luck will be
Until of flies you swat fifty-
three.*

There's a morsel of validity in the
encouragement not to kill house
spiders, at least in ancient times.
Before the invention of insecticide
sprays, spiders helped keep down
the number of household flies, thus
lessening the risks of disease. Having
let the spider live, then if you see a spider running across
one of your garments, this signifies that good fortune
will bring you new clothes. And if a spider suddenly
abseils from the ceiling onto you (it happens!) rejoice —
something good is about to occur, possibly financially!

One of the oldest superstitions of all is that if you kill a
spider, rain will come. This may be perceived as either
good or bad, depending on where you live and local
crop requirements at the time. In parts of America it is
considered unlucky to see a spider in the morning. If so,
it should be killed immediately. But by noon the spider
has become a harbinger of joy, and by evening the sight of
one represents hope.

But certainly hunt out a live spider if your temperature
is feverish. Tucking the spider into a spoonful of jam and
eating both is believed to bring your temperature down.
Moreover, spiders' webs collected, squashed into a
pill-shaped lump and swallowed will (hopefully) relieve
asthma. Myth-makers were not confined to enhancing
Christian imagery. Muslims tell an exact replica of the
spider spinning a web across a cave mouth and causing
searching soldiers to bypass it, but in the Muslim version
it is Muhammad hiding from his enemies inside the cave.

See also **cobweb**; **asthma**.

a 'mortal' form. For this reason, ejection of part of oneself was seen as pleasing the 'gods' by warning away any lurking evil and instead inviting favourable circumstances. Let us remember that a blind man's sight was restored by Jesus with his saliva (Mark 8:23).

The power of spit still crops up in circumstances where good luck is being sought. A discreet spit can sometimes be deposited on playing cards before a game; on boxing gloves before a bout; on exam papers before the gong rings; on golf balls before a match; and even a light spit on the hands before shaking another hand — to emphasise that a business deal is legitimate and/or a promise will be kept. Spitting on the hands also 'bestows' a strength when preparing to dig or fight.

The really dedicated superstition buff will discreetly spit on their finger if they see a cross-eyed person or a magpie. An even more passionate devotee will spit on their fingernails and hair clippings before disposing of them in order to prevent witches from stealing them for spell-making. And there's more: spit on the right shoe before embarking on a journey; spit on the field before bringing a crop in; and spit in new clothes before putting them on.

Clearly those who follow all of the spit superstitions must have to suck a lot of throat lozenges.

splinter

A superstition concerning the humble splinter seems likely to have arisen out of a deep sense of faith, combined with the imagination to create a new 'biblical' story (which isn't actually in the Bible). First published in *Defensative against the Poyson of supposed Prophecies* (1583), the following rhyme is to be said over an impaled splinter or thorn:

Our Lord was the fyrst man

That ever thorne prickt upon;
It never blysted, nor it never belted*,
And I pray God nor this not may.

(*belted: turned evil colours, presaging infection)

It was believed that reciting the verse over the splintered area would cause the splinter to slide out of the flesh and into open air, with no septic after-effects.

Of course one undoubtedly needed deep faith for this to work. If lacking conviction, there was another possibility. An ancient remedy to get rid of a splinter was to bind it with a poultice of donkey dung.

spoon

Through no effort of its own, the domestic spoon became the target of several ancient superstitions.

If a spoon drops and lands with its bowl upwards, then expect a happy surprise. But if the bowl lands downwards, a major disappointment lies ahead. There is/was also a belief that bad luck attended anyone who stirred with a spoon in the left hand (no leeway given to those born left-handed).

Curiously, spoons made of wood developed completely opposing symbolisms. Centuries before microwave ovens and stainless steel cookware, a wooden spoon was regarded as one of the most useful things a young wife could have in her kitchen, so it was a popular traditional gift for a bride. In reverse, a wooden spoon was regarded by students at Cambridge University in the early 1800s as the most useless of objects, and was thus ceremoniously awarded to those who had the lowest marks in Honours degree examinations.

From this there gradually grew and spread the concept of a 'wooden spoon' being given to either (a) the runner-up in a

contest, or (b) the person who comes last. In some cases it is
simply a case of applying the term to them; at other times the
real thing is handed over.

sprains

Most folk who have a sprained ankle or wrist seek guidance from
a physiotherapist, with perhaps some restrictive bandaging and
help with household chores. But to regain normal joint flexibility,
the superstitious have other treatments. One is to find a piece
of string from a flour bag and tie it around the area, or more
effectively, wrap the joint in the skin of an eel.

stairs

Various superstitions have arisen about going up and down
stairs, perhaps originating from those narrow and perilous
medieval stairs built on the inside of steep stone walls, with no
handrail and rudimentary light.

Meeting someone going the opposite way was very bad. Doom and
gloom would eventuate if you met someone going up or coming
down. One way to avert disaster was to cross fingers immediately
when the usurper was spotted.

Catching your foot or tripping had two significances. If it
happened on the way down it was the herald of bad luck on the
way. But tripping when going upwards brought the likelihood of
a wedding soon (not necessarily for the tripper if he or she was
already married, but for someone close to them).

But worst of all was being on the staircase halfway and
remembering something left behind, then turning back and
retracing one's own steps up or down. How to overcome such a
potentially disastrous situation? Easy — sit down and whistle for
a few moments. The evil omen will be cancelled out.

stars

The belief that stars have some significance to human destiny
has been a major factor throughout recorded history. At least
two aspects of these ancient beliefs survive in the modern
world.

Today, studying the position of the stars and interpreting their
influence on the lives of people born within designated divisions
of the year provide guidance to thousands of people who believe,
as did many of the ancients, that the planetary system governs
lifestyle, romance and good fortune (or otherwise). Usually
known as astrology, early forms of the study and its beliefs date
back at least two millennia BC, though considerable refinements
have evolved over the centuries, resulting eventually in popular
newspaper horoscopes.

Another less complex survivor from the ancients is the belief that
making a silent wish when the stars perform in a certain way will
help make the wish come true. The basis for this belief appears to
have been known as far back as c.AD 51 and probably earlier. The
Greek astronomer Ptolemy reported a belief that the (Greek) gods
on high occasionally moved a star or two aside out of curiosity
in order to look down through the gap at how earthlings actually
lived. During these brief rearrangements, the star-moving which
occurred could be seen from down below and became known as
'shooting stars'. Their movement indicated that the gods were
available through a gap and thus could be approached directly, so
it was a good time to send up a wish!

Over several centuries this was modified. Some still believe it
appropriate to make a wish when seeing a shooting star, but a
more common belief is to make a wish when seeing the first star
on any night. A rhyme associated with this belief (superstition?)
may have originated in Yorkshire, before surfacing in America.
The earliest known example in print is in Will de Grasse's
'Swallows on the wing o'er garden springs of delight' (1866):

Star light, star bright
The first star I have seen tonight
I wish I may
I wish I might
Have the wish I have wished tonight . . .

The concept of wishing on a star surfaced in the movie *The Wizard of Oz* (1939) when Judy Garland sang endearingly of life over a rainbow:

Some day I'll wish upon a star, and wake up where the clouds are far behind me . . .

A year later in Walt Disney's movie *Pinocchio* (1940) the concept of wishing on a star made an even greater impact. The elderly puppet-maker Geppetto was seen peering out the window and reciting the 'Star light, star bright' poem with the wish that Pinocchio could become a real boy. Jiminy Cricket enlarged on the suggestion with the enchanting song 'When you wish upon a star'.

swallows

In countries inhabited by the swallow it is seen as a harbinger of summer, but it is also attended by some conflicting 'beliefs'. At the crucifixion did the swallows:
(a) cry out 'Dead dead' over the suffering Jesus to prevent soldiers from torturing him further?
Or:
(b) fly around the suffering Jesus and cry 'Cheer up Cheer up'?

The latter is believed in Sweden, the former elsewhere, but neither has any support from the Bible itself.

swans

It has sometimes been believed that if you kill a swan, your own death will occur soon after. But if instead of killing it you take

step on a crack

'. . . and break your mother's back.' This saying is thought to have become current in the late nineteenth century (and clearly after footpaths and streets became paved). American versions of the superstition had unpleasant racist references:

Step on a crack, and your mother will turn black.
Step on a crack, your mother's baby will be black.

Equally unpleasant is this variation:

Step on a crack, your mother's a rat.

Fortunately, public sensitivity eventually restored the saying to its former shape, referring to the cracks in pavements as leading to 'the underworld', and stepping on them would release the evil spirits dwelling below. Variations include:

Step on a line, break your mother's spine.
Step on a hole, break your mother's sugar bowl.
Step on a nail, you'll put your dad in jail.

An alternative (and much later) superstition warning children not to step on the cracks was the fear that wild bears would attack them if they did (thought to have arisen from A. A. Milne's poem 'Lines and Squares').

just one feather from a swan, it can help provide marital calm, because a swan's feather, sewn into a husband's pillow, will ensure fidelity.

There is a common belief that swans only sing when dying. And although hardly a superstition, this ingrained belief is totally without any basis in fact, so it comes close to qualifying. It was 458 BC when the Greek dramatist Aeschylus mentioned that swans sang as they died. Plato reported that Socrates believed swans sang beautifully before they died, and Aristotle agreed. However, Pliny the Elder was of sterner stuff and declared in AD 77 that their 'singing whilst dying' was a total myth. But too late — for nearly 2500 years the earlier belief reigned, and the contradiction was ignored by Chaucer, Shakespeare and Tennyson. The English language acquired and still uses the word 'swansong', alluding to the fact that swan-singing indicates the end, the last stage of a career or process.

So the misconception lingers on, but like a superstition, it is 'above reality'.

table

According to superstition, a number of dire consequences can be provoked by actions associated with this humble domestic object.

- Do not move from your allocated seat to another seat — bad luck will descend upon you.
- Be careful never to kick over your chair — it is the sign of a liar.
- Never sing while at a table . . . it presages your early death.
- Never lie down upon a table . . . ditto.
- Leaving a tablecloth on all night until morning can cause only bad things.
- If you want evil to bypass you, never put shoes on a table.
- If you've just eaten your first meal at another person's table, folding your napkin at the end of the meal indicates that you will never be asked there again.
- If pie is being served, cut in triangular slices American-style, don't start eating at the pointed end, for that will bring misfortune.
- If children crawl beneath the table, their untimely death may be near — unless they crawl out from under the table at exactly the place they crawled in.
- Single young women must avoid sitting at a table corner — it will jeopardise their chances of marrying.

- If a piece of table cutlery is dropped, it must be picked up by someone else, not the dropper.
- If the cutlery dropped is a carving knife, prepare for an imminent visit from a policeman.
- If it is a fork, someone's engagement will soon be broken.

Fortunately none of the above applies to picnic cloths spread on the ground, or lap trays in front of the television.

tea

As with tables, the common and popular cup of tea is beset with major significances.

Accidentally spilling some of the leaves while loading the pot portends good things (though it's not valid if done deliberately — and not possible anyway with teabags). Stirring tea within the pot should be avoided — especially anti-clockwise. And the lid must always be on the pot — leaving it off could cause quarrels. If the tea is too strong, friendship will develop among those drinking, but if too weak, there could be a falling-out among the party.

A single woman who likes milk and sugar is advised to put the sugar in first — if milk is added first it will nullify her chances of marriage. Unless of course a man pours her a cup of tea — and soon after pours her a *second* cup, in which case she is well on the way to being seduced by him (though not necessarily married).

At the end of drinking, tasseography (aka tasseomancy) can take over — the interpretation of one's character and future by the disposition of tea leaves. Its origins date back to medieval times, when it was done with other substances, but it transferred to tea leaves in the 1600s. A journey, an inheritance, a wedding, good and bad luck — all can be 'read' in the used and leftover leaves (again, not possible with teabags). When it's all over, one belief is that all used tea leaves ('read' or not) should be thrown in front of the house to help ward off evil spirits.

See also **coffee**.

Thanksgiving

This major American holiday dates from a gathering of 53 settlers and twice that number of Native Americans in 1621. Only one eye-witness account exists — a letter written by Edward Winslow, who described the event not so much as a solemn occasion of thanks, but more as a harvest festival:

that we might after a special manner rejoice together after we had gathered the fruit of our labours.

But over centuries people came to appreciate the enormous faith the early settlers had shown by journeying to the unknown and unsettled land, and the later realisation of what the land had to offer them. So the concept of a Thanksgiving commemoration developed. It became official in 1863 when Abraham Lincoln proclaimed that Thanksgiving Day would be the last Thursday in November every year.

Customs which now surround Thanksgiving include two which are classified as 'superstitions' and one which bears a relationship to ancient forms of Gifting the Sovereign:

- If the person who prepares the (usually lavish) Thanksgiving meal does so alone without the help of others, and also does not own their own house, they will own one within a year.
- Whoever cooks the Thanksgiving turkey must knock three times on a wooden surface before putting the bird in the oven. The knocking will ensure it is cooked to tenderness.

Then there is the matter of the Presidential Pardon for a turkey. In 1947 the National Turkey Federation presented a prize turkey to the president, and has continued to do so every year since. The

thirteen

The superstition around this number has a powerful reputation — and one to which big business pays attention. Consider the restaurants which have no table labelled 13, the airlines with no row 13 seating, and multistorey hotels which do not have a thirteenth floor (well they do, of course, but it's probably numbered 12A) and room numbers which jump from 12 to 14.

Furthermore, in 2015 the *Daily Mail* reported that houses in Britain numbered 13 in their street sold for significantly lower prices than their immediate neighbours, and that house sales customarily drop by a third on the 13th of any month. Some councils in Britain have banned number 13 altogether — 28 percent of streets in the UK have no number 13. London's famous Downing Street has twenty houses, but none of them is numbered 13.

So how did the superstition that 13 is an unlucky number arise?

It was known to be suspect in ancient Roman times. But not only in Rome. Ancient Norse mythology tells the story of Baldur, god of beauty, life and truth, who invited eleven guests for an evening of celebration in Valhalla, when the mischievous god Loki walked in uninvited — bringing the number in the room to thirteen. Loki had been told that Baldur was impervious to any weapon made from natural vegetation — except mistletoe. Loki found some mistletoe, and in devil-may-care spirit he persuaded Hod, the old god of darkness, who was blind, to shoot an arrow into the air to test Baldur's famed resistance to any kind of wood. But Loki had tipped the arrow with mistletoe and magically guided Hod's aim towards Baldur. When it hit him, Baldur died, the earth became dark and the gods became sure that Ragnarok, the end of the cosmos, was near. From then on, the number 13 became ominous and full of foreboding.

A much later connection links thirteen with the night before Jesus prepared for the Passover, when twelve people sat down with him at his Seder meal, and that grouping of thirteen was the last moment of peace before the start of events with massive future influence.

So take your pick. There's even a word for it — fear of the number 13 is officially known as triskaidekaphobia.

See also **Black Friday**; **mistletoe**; **twelve**.

impression was given that having been presented with the turkey, the president and his family should eat it, which apparently Truman and many of his successors did. But in 1987 President Reagan made the gesture of 'pardoning' the gift bird, sparing its life and sending it to retire on a turkey farm. In 1988 Reagan's successor, President George Bush, made the pardoning an annual official ceremony, as have presidents since, freeing the birds from their destiny of being killed and eaten. They are now sent to take part in the annual Disney Thanksgiving Parade, and then to live out the rest of their natural life.

three — a lucky number?

The often uttered phrase 'third time lucky' is a superstition whose origins are thought to be grounded in the Christian Trinity. Alas, in parallel with its lucky aura, 'three' also exists as a superstition of the obverse — that accidents, disasters and funerals 'come in threes'.

thumb

It's the most mundane of digits, but it is the subject of a widespread superstition that should the thumb show signs of itchiness, an unexpected visitor will soon arrive. Shakespeare's version in Macbeth gives added value when one of the witches announces:

By the pricking of my thumbs, something wicked this way comes . . .

thunder

An obscure and centuries-old superstition of British origin handily predicts what will happen when thunder occurs on each day of the week:

Monday advises that a woman will die.

Tuesday presages a good grain harvest.
Wednesday warns of approaching social violence.
Thursday declares the farmers' livestock will flourish.
Friday thunder means a battle is about to be fought.
Saturday is worse — an epidemic is coming soon.
Sunday thunder indicates a prominent citizen is about to die.

thyme

This innocent herb, with its faint but unique fragrance, is somewhat unfairly associated with at least three troublesome events.

For no known reason — but when did superstition ever need a reason? — some devotees of the supernatural believe that when the scent of thyme is detected in the presence of a death, then the scent is telling us the death was not natural — it was murder!

Still on the theme of death, we can choose to follow the belief that thyme's tiny flowers form a safe harbour in which the souls of the dead can rest in peace. It's a sobering thought if one chooses to believe it, because in stuffing the Christmas turkey, the aforementioned safe harbours of the departed would be firmly disturbed, even destroyed, as thyme joins the sage and breadcrumbs inside the soon-to-be-roasted festive bird.

On a slightly more positive note, there is a superstition that thyme can increase levels of courage and therefore help counter depression. If there is truth in this, a battalion of genuine medical consultants could be out of work.

See also **marigold**.

toast, drinking a

The name comes from a centuries-old practice of putting a small piece of actual toast into drinks in the belief that it improved the flavour. Shakespeare's Falstaff mentions it:

Go fetch me a quart of sack; put a toast in't.

It has been mooted (though it's of questionable veracity) that drinking a toast to someone is so that the assembly, in drinking a sip before the guest of honour drinks, can be assured that the guest is not going to be poisoned. But history shows that the ancient Greeks would offer libations to the gods as a ritualistic practice, as well as drinking to each other's health. *The Odyssey* relates that Ulysses drank to the health of Achilles, and some Roman emperors were 'drunk to' at every meal.

But superstition kicks in when it comes to the clinking of glasses, either as part of the toast ritual or in many other social situations. Why do we clink glasses? The clinking noise scares and sends away any evil spirits who may be lurking at the occasion.

tombstone

In his study of funeral history and practices, *Beyond the Grave*, social researcher of history and the supernatural, Troy Taylor, explains that tombstones were originally not a marker and memorial of the late departed. Their purpose was much more mundane. Primitive superstition held that under some circumstances the dead might arise and cause mayhem among the living. To avoid this, the burial place was weighed down with a heavy stone or boulders to keep the dead safely interred. Moving the stone's position to the head of the grave and inscribing it came much later.

twelve

Numerologists consider 12 to be a number which signifies 'a

touch wood

This mild demonstration of hope, that by 'touching wood' any unfortunate effects resulting from whatever has been said or done might be nullified, has its origin in a centuries-old belief that guiding spirits lived inside trees. Acknowledging the spirit's presence by touching the wood meant that the spirit within would return the courtesy by ensuring good would come of what you'd hoped for — or that nothing bad would result if your wish had been apprehensive. When, as frequently happened, there was a lack of forest trees, touching any old piece of wood came to be acceptable as a replacement.

After the emergence of Christianity, a new interpretation of the practice was filtered into place, that saying 'touch wood' was a momentary appeal to the cross on which Jesus was crucified, thus hopefully connecting with his or its power to help. In the more recent era of plastic and lamination, saying the words is easy, but finding some wood nearby to touch can be a problem. Hence it has become customary to believe that just saying the words, without necessarily touching anything, will invoke the same form of intervention by the supernatural as it did in centuries past.

completed cycle of experience' and has the aura of harmony. There are 12 months in a year, the day is divided into 12 hours, the zodiac has 12 signs, Olympus had 12 gods, there were 12 labours of Hercules, 12 tribes of Israel and 12 apostles of Jesus. The number 13, because it exceeds 12 by 1, may be perceived with uneasiness because it is just a little beyond completeness. It is 'unbalanced'.

See also **thirteen**.

twins

Some ancient cultures viewed twins with great suspicion. It was as if their being born outside the norm of 'one pregnancy, one birth' indicated their mother's evil association with an interfering alien spirit.

Slightly more benign, but demonstrably naïve, was a superstition that twins occurred not because of anything evil, but because of something much more mundane — that the father had spilt some pepper at some time during his wife's pregnancy. This of course flies in the face of the later proven fact that twinship is established at the moment of conception, not after the pregnancy has been initiated.

tying the knot

The commonly used phrase 'tying the knot' dates back to an ancient Babylonic superstition that a bridal union is final when some threads are pulled from the bride's clothes and the groom's and tied together. The practice has gone into abeyance but the expression remains.

U

Some people like to include the letter U in their lives in various ways — for example, in the name of their house or in a car number-plate — since it most resembles a lucky horseshoe.

ulcers

In times past, mouth ulcers were perceived to be the result of telling lies. Two treatments were available to those who did not have recourse to modern medicine:

⊚ Stand with the sufferer three times a day and read aloud Psalm 8, which includes the phrase 'out of the mouths of babes and sucklings'.

⊚ Eat a dog's tongue.

The one practical treatment known to subdue mouth ulcers was (and still is) the application of an evilly unpleasant tincture made from bitter myrrh — its only apparent use. Why this was given to a baby, along with gold and frankincense, is a question never satisfactorily answered.

umbrella

The name is descended from the Latin diminutive *umbra*, meaning shade or shadow. For many centuries umbrellas were solely for protection from the sun. It wasn't until the 1700s that it seemed to occur to anyone that they could also protect from rain.

umbilical cord

In some cultures the placenta and its umbilical cord are buried with great care. No longer in use once the baby is born, it is respected for keeping the unborn child protected and nourished, and therefore some rules were established concerning its possible effect on the child's later life:

- If the cord is burned, it is feared the child will die in fire one day.
- If thrown into water, there is a danger of future drowning.
- Burial in the ground is the wise choice — under roses if possible, or near a strong vine — to send vibes of health and strength to the growing infant.
- Alternatively, some elect to keep the cord, dried and in a small bag, and wear it discreetly under clothes to encourage evil spirits to go and bother someone else.

Naturally, superstitions gathered around them. The most common of them was not to open an umbrella inside the house — something bad will come of it. Nor must it ever be laid — even unfurled — on a bed or a table.

And any woman yet unmarried who drops her umbrella must wait for someone else to pick it up. If she retrieves it herself, she will never wed.

unicorns

So far, no unicorns have ever been found. Nevertheless, among the superstitions surrounding them is one that causes hope in the hearts of those still seeking them, namely that powdered unicorn horn makes a highly effective aphrodisiac.

urine

Some curious rituals and beliefs surround this ubiquitous fluid. Because of its intimate association with those who originate it, urine must always be protected from being stolen by witches, who might cast evil spells over the urine producer. To ward off witches with urine-theft in mind, precautions include scattering some urine on the door-frames of the house. And if witchery is suspected to be happening already, it can be stopped in its tracks by baking a cake with urine in the recipe.

And pre-dating cell phones, an ancient belief can help a household keep in touch with a family member on a long journey. The secret is to keep some of the traveller's urine back home in a jar. The traveller's welfare can then be monitored. If the urine continues to be clear, the absent one's well-being is not in doubt. But should it turn cloudy, an emergency of some kind has occurred and the traveller must be rescued.

See also **deafness**; **sage**.

vampires

Do they exist?

The first known 'vampire story' published in English was *The Vampyre*, a short work of prose fiction written in 1819 by John William Polidori. But Bram Stoker's later tale, *Dracula* (1897), certainly made a bigger impact, which continues to this day. Over 150 movies have been made in the vampire genre inspired by Bram Stoker and his Dracula.

It's possible to believe that vampires did or still do exist, though those who believe it are fairly rare.

See also **garlic**.

Voodoo

Though not of American origin, the supernatural beliefs collectively known as Voodoo came to be a recognised part of America's spiritual landscape. The template was a combined interpretation of basic African beliefs, influenced by the circumstances in which black people from Africa found themselves when taken into slavery in Louisiana, where they came into contact with the strong religious beliefs of Spanish and French settlers.

The various racial mixes known as Creole formulated customs based on superstitions which sometimes combined elements from the old world of Europe with influences from neighbouring Haiti and South America, and eventually gained a strongly American character. Based on its cultural mix of languages and differing religious beliefs, Voodoo integrated such elements as spirit and ancestor worship, plus herbs, poison, amulets and *fetiches* — charms believed to have magical powers (which could be made of feathers, bones, crystals, cut-off hair or a creature's foot) — or a specially made doll. Used correctly, Voodoo practices could influence life and its events. Here are some of its beliefs:

- A combination of ancient German belief and Voodoo could cause a person you don't like a great disfavour. Sneaking into their pillow a fetiche of rags, bones and hair, suitably 'charmed,' would cause the enemy great discomfort.
- This however could be averted by the recipient taking the precaution of always sleeping with an open pair of scissors under the pillow.
- A broom is for sweeping the floor — and that's all. If the broom touches anyone other than the sweeper, the other person feels badly cursed and must arrange for the broom to be spat on immediately to allay the evil.
- A charm or fetiche is laid before a house entrance or single room and some oil is poured around it. Whoever crosses the oil is going to be badly affected by the fetiche. But this can be cancelled out by obtaining some sand or salt (without crossing the oil to get inside) and sprinkling it on the oil to nullify its effect.
- If a visitor to a house doesn't make a favourable impression, salt is scattered by the door after the visitor has left, then swept firmly away. The visitor will never return.
- A girl who steps on a cat's tail will not be married until at least one year has elapsed.
- Seeing a white butterfly is good luck.
- If two marriages are celebrated in one occasion, one of the husbands will soon die.

warts

Among various superstitious remedies, a special one recommended by the faithful has some social and legal difficulties. Namely, warts will disappear when rubbed with bacon which *must have been stolen* — ordinary supermarket-bought bacon won't work.

Less trouble is likely to be caused by another ancient 'cure': to rub the warts with the inner surface of an empty bean pod. Alternatively, Pliny's *Natural History* (AD 79) advises touching each wart with a different pea on the first day of a new moon, then wrapping the peas in a cloth and throwing the bundle away — backwards.

Or for a somewhat unsympathetic cure, rub a frog over the warts, then impale the frog on a tree and leave it to die.

wedding ring

The circular ring shape has long represented eternity. It is believed that several centuries BC, rings were made of dried and braided reeds, signifying the hope that a marriage would be long-lasting. Some branches of Christianity adapted the ring's significance to represent the eternity of God, who has no beginning and no end, and a wedding ring became a standard element in Christian weddings.

wedding cake

There is an old superstition that the more rich
and tasty the wedding cake is, the more fertile and
abundant the marriage will be. But bear this in mind:
if the first cake baked for the wedding is a failure, the
marriage will be a failure.

In ancient times, there was a superstition that after
the ceremony and towards the end of the socialising,
one way of encouraging marital good luck was to break
the wedding cake over the bride's head, after which the
guests sprinkled all the broken bits and crumbs over
their own heads. Curiously, this old superstition has
not survived into the modern era. More likely the cake
will be sedately sliced, superstition decreeing that the
first slice be cut by the bride to ensure the marriage
will not be childless, but in these times of equality the
groom customarily places his hand on top of hers.

If the cake is tiered, a
sensibly superstitious bride
will keep one tier (or a
slice if it is one-level).
This will — or to be
honest, *might* — ensure
that children will come to
the marriage and the husband
will remain faithful.

An unmarried wedding guest can
keep her slice of wedding cake
and sleep with it under her pillow
— if she wants to dream about the
identity of her future partner.

Ancient Egyptians believed that a special blood vein led from the heart straight to the third finger of the left hand, so the wedding ring was worn there. Although the belief about the significant vein was later proved to be completely false, the superstition took hold and millions of people still wear their wedding ring on their left third finger. However, in some cultures it is worn on the right hand: Serbia, Hungary, Greece, Ukraine, Norway, Spain and others.

Another superstitious belief decrees that if a wedding ring is turned round the finger three times while making a wish, the wish will come true.

weeds

According to an ancient piece of folklore, weeds exist as a result of a curse laid on the soil by God after the disobedience of Adam. The Rev. Foster Barham Zincke, chaplain to Queen Victoria, wasn't so sure. He wrote in 1892:

I have heard confidently announced as if there could be no doubt about it, that weeds are natural to the ground, in the sense that the ground originates them; and that no man ever did, because no man ever could, eradicate them. They spring eternal from the ground itself, not at all necessarily from the seeds of parent weeds . . .

To this ignorance is superadded in the case of weeds a theological conception, that the ground has been cursed with weeds as a punishment for man's disobedience. It has therefore ever borne, and will ever continue to bear thistles and speargrass. It is then useless, not to say that it is a sign of a rebellious spirit, to attempt to clean one's land thoroughly. It is pious to accept this dispensation up to a certain point.

window

There is a belief among the Creole people of Louisiana that a mother should never pass her child through a window (presumably to someone else on the other side), because to do so will stunt the child's growth.

wishbones

Paying attention to wishbones can be traced back to the Etruscans, an ancient Italian civilisation. The Etruscans believed that hens held prophetic powers, and they would perform a ritual called alectryomancy, or 'rooster divination'. One or more hens (or roosters) were placed in the middle of a circle divided into wedges (one for each letter of the alphabet). Bits of food were scattered on each section and scribes would take note of each wedge from which the hens snacked. The letters were then taken to the local priests, who would use the information to answer the city's questions about the future. (It was like an ancient live Ouija board.)

After the oracle, a hen was killed and its wishbone (or *furcula*) was laid out in the sun to be preserved. People would come to stroke and wish on the bone, believing it to retain the powers of the living chicken.

The Romans eventually picked up this tradition, but gave it their own twist. Due to a high demand for the bones, two people would share one and break it in half. The larger half had the greater propensity for good fortune and prophetic powers. Author Charles Panati, former professor of industrial physics and science editor of *Newsweek*, points out that the expression 'a lucky break' is sometimes attributed to this ancient practice and its attendant superstition.

worms

This is definitely an unwelcome affliction, and it has its very own superstition to cure it. Take a hair from a horse's forelock, place it between two slices of buttered bread and eat the horsehair sandwich.

Xmas

To some people, the custom of writing the word Christmas
as Xmas is seen as offensive to the Christ figure, and some
superstitiously avoid doing so. In fact it is not a custom of
laziness but a perfectly respectable and valid abbreviation, and
has been in use for centuries.

The word Christ was never part of Jesus' name — it is a title
meaning 'the anointed one', or in other words 'the messiah'. In
ancient Greece the letter *chi* was written with a symbol very like
a modern X, and the title assigned to Jesus — Xristos — was
frequently abbreviated to just X. So both Christmas and Xmas
can be translated as 'the mass for the anointed messiah'. In
English, the written form Xmas has been used without disrespect
since 1551 (but should be pronounced 'Christmas' rather than
'Ex-mas').

yawn

It is generally understood that the reason a hand discreetly covers a yawn is politeness: to protect onlookers from an unexpected Cinemascope of your open mouth and its insides. But the custom is actually the result of an ancient superstition.

The ancients believed that, as with sneezing, a yawn could be an avenue for the body's essential elements — its life and its soul — to escape. Quickly positioning a hand over the (virtually uncontrollable) yawning mouth ensured that the soul and life spirit were being held back inside. In addition, the hand-cover was a protection against hovering evil persons such as the Devil himself, who might take the opportunity to go right in. The element of politeness came later.

Bibliography

Many sources were used in the preparation of this work. The following works were of special assistance:

Brasch, R., *How Did It Begin?* Collins, Sydney, 1988.

Encyclopaedia Britannica (15th edition). London, 2010.

Haining, Peter, *Superstitions*. Sidgwick & Jackson, London, 1979.

Panati, Charles, *Extraordinary Origins of Everyday Things*. Harper & Row, New York, 1987.

Pickering, David, *Dictionary of Superstition*. Cassell, London, 2002.

Radford, E. and M. A. (ed. and rev. Christina Hole), *The Encyclopaedia of Superstitions*. Hutchinson & Co, London, 1961.

Webster, Richard, *The Encyclopaedia of Superstitions*. Llewellyn Publications, Woodbury (Minnesota), 2008.

If you enjoyed this book, you will love these other books by Max Cryer:

Curious English Words and Phrases:
The truth behind the expressions we use.
Informative and entertaining, this is a treasure trove for lovers of language, as Max Cryer dispels myths and uncovers meanings. From 'couch potato' to 'Bob's your uncle', you'll find the explanation here.

Preposterous Proverbs:
Why fine words butter no parsnips.
With his characteristic wry wit, Max Cryer looks at a vast array of proverbs from around the world, analysing the origin and meaning behind some of the most interesting and perplexing proverbs.

Who Said That First?:
The curious origins of common words and phrases.
In this very readable book, Max Cryer explores the origins of hundreds of expressions we use and hear every day — with some surprising findings. Written in his delightfully witty style.

Every Dog Has Its Day: A thousand things you didn't know about man's best friend.
This superb collection tells the stories of famous dogs, explains the origins of some of our favourite breeds, describes the surprising activities in which dogs are involved and how dogs have infiltrated our language.

The Cat's Out of the Bag: Truth and lies about cats.
Everything you ever wanted to know about cats can be found in this splendid book: their unique attributes; their special place in many cultures; how they have influenced our language; famous cat characters; cats with celebrity owners.

Is It True?:
The facts behind the things we have been told.
The surprising truths behind some of our most cherished beliefs are revealed in this entertaining book, from politics, science and social history to language, music and the natural world.

Love books? Love words? Visit www.wordbooks.com.au

EXISLE
PUBLISHING

www.exislepublishing.com